The Game is Up

Book 4

We believe that the Bible is God's word to mankind, and that it contains everything we need to know in order to be reconciled with God and live in a way that is pleasing to him. Therefore, we believe it is vital to teach children accurately from the Bible, being careful to teach each passage's true meaning in an appropriate way for children, rather than selecting a 'children's message' from a Biblical passage.

29 Buxton Gardens, Acton, London, W3 9LE
Tel: 020 8992 0450

Contributors: Trevor Blundell; Thalia Blundell; Annie Gemmill; Guy Lachlan; Kirsteen McCulloch

Published by Christian Focus Publications Ltd
Geanies House, Fearn, Tain, Ross-shire, IV20 1TW
Tel: 01862 871 011 Fax: 01862 871 699
email: info@christianfocus.com

Cover design by Tim Charnick
Illustrations by Tim Charnick
Printed by Arrowsmith

This book and others in the series can be purchased from your local Christian bookshop. Alternatively you can write to TnT Ministries direct or place your order with the publisher.

ISBN 1-85792-821-0

TnT Ministries (which stands for Teaching and Training Ministries) was launched in February 1993 by Christians from a broad variety of denominational backgrounds who are concerned that teaching the Bible to children be taken seriously. The leaders were in charge of a Sunday School of 50 teachers at St Helen's Bishopgate, an evangelical church in the city of London, for 13 years, during which time a range of Biblical teaching material has been developed. TnT Ministries also runs training days for Sunday School teachers.

Contents

Introduction

The great desire of our hearts is that children everywhere will come to love and trust Jesus as their Lord and Saviour. It is our firm belief that this happens primarily through the teaching of God's word in the Bible. This book of games and ideas is designed as a resource to complement and support Bible teaching. It has been written as a companion volume to the 'On the Way' Bible teaching programme, but is suitable for use in any situation where the Bible is being taught to children.

Teaching the Bible is an exacting task. Teaching the Bible to children is even more so. The concepts are sometimes hard to communicate and are often contrary to the norms in the secular society in which they live. They are used to an interactive style of learning and they want to have fun. Traditionally we have tended to separate off the 'Bible teaching' slot from the rest of the activities in our children's programmes which are fun but have no Bible content. How much better to make every part of the programme count in the teaching of God's word! Since children learn by repetition, why teach something once when you can teach it several times, using all the activities and games to contribute to the learning process? In this way not only is learning enhanced but the Bible is exciting, relevant and truly central to the group's activities.

In this book we have outlined 3 supplementary activities - the Warm Up, the Consolidation and the Wind Up. Though this is only one model of an integrated teaching approach, it has been used by TnT Ministries with great success for many years. We have found consistently that with this kind of repetition even the smallest child can learn big things about God.

Warm Up

This is a short activity or presentation designed to arrest the attention of the children and prepare them for the Bible teaching which is to follow.

Consolidation

This is a constructive game or activity designed to reinforce the key concepts, theme, aim or details of the Bible story that has just been taught. It generally involves plenty of physical activity and some simple equipment.

Wind Up

A Wind Up is the final summation of the days teaching. It involves linking the Warm Up, the Bible story and the Consolidation together, emphasising the central teaching point.

Warm ups and wind ups take around 5 minutes and a Consolidation game 10-15 minutes. For each Bible story there are 2 schemes of Warm Ups, Consolidations and Wind Ups described. One will often require more space or more equipment. The ideas and suggestions in this book are only guidelines for you to adapt and change in line with the age, number and needs of your children and limitations of your meeting space. We would stress that they should be used alongside, not in place of, teaching directly from the Bible. In some warm ups the leader demonstrates negative qualities, such as favouritism. When acting out of character we suggest that you don a hat or jacket, or call yourself a different name, so that the younger children do not equate the bad points with the leader.

The Purpose of Miracles

Many New Testament stories deal with miracles. It is important that the children are taught clearly the difference between miracles and magic. Miracles show God restoring or creating in line with his nature and are signs that God is at work. They take place when God acts in the natural order in an unusual manner and their occurrence are predicted and/or take place at the command or prayer of God's messenger.

The purpose of miracles is:

- to bring glory to God (John 2:11; 11:4)
- to authenticate the ministry of the person performing them (John 3:2)
- to lead the observer(s) to faith in God (John 20:30-31, Acts 9:36-42)
- to deepen the faith of the believers.

True miracles always harmonise with the rest of Scripture in their portrayal of God's character. Magic, on the other hand, is always to do with illusion and deception. i.e. to trick or fool the observer(s).

Creating your own Games

Why not create your own games, custom made to serve your children, and take advantage of the special possibilities of your meeting place? It's easy if you take account of a few basic principles. The first task is to spend time in the Bible. Your game is a teaching opportunity and you need to understand the message of your passage for the day before you will know the concept, aim or details you want to teach from it via the game. There are four important elements to designing and running successful games.

Rules

There need to be SIMPLE RULES which are easily understood and which can be enforced to make the game fun, safe, workable and educational.

- Explain the rules, then ask questions to see if they have understood them. Then ask if they have any questions before repeating the rules and starting the game. This may sound laborious but it is a good investment of time.
- Start the game with a clear command, e.g. 'When I say GO', or, 'When I drop my hand'.
- The rules must be applied consistently and rule breakers need to be dealt with firmly.

Participation

Games are for joining in, not for watching, and so good games involve lots of participation. To make a game fun for everyone, as many children as possible need to be on the move at the same time. However, a safe environment must be preserved at all times.

- Games involving cross movements of children or games depending on speed alone are best avoided.
- Small or otherwise vulnerable children must be protected. Sometimes it is possible to design a game where these children have a different role from the older ones. All children should be encouraged to take part but never forced.
- It is wise to have a strategy for stopping the game and restoring order if necessary. The command 'Statues' or 'Freeze' will do this. A 'Sin Bin' is also useful for rule breakers.

A Scoring System

A scoring system is needed to determine who wins. Children are naturally competitive and learning to win and lose graciously is a valuable social skill. However:

- It must be absolutely fair and administered by an impartial adult.
- It must be understandable, preferably visual.
- All efforts should be affirmed and congratulated. A running commentary by the game leader is very helpful.

Equipment

Equipment of some sort is needed for nearly all games. Children like to hold, carry and hide things.

- Almost anything can be used in games, but it must be safe. It is unwise to include anything which might be used as a weapon.
- It should be easy to reset if necessary during the game and easy to clear up at the end.
- The ideal is to have a small store of safe, versatile items for use in your games.

List of suggested items

Balloons & blow-up items	Empty plastic soft drink bottles	Soft sponge balls
Balls of string	Newspapers	Sponges
Buckets	Small items to act as tokens	Table tennis balls
Cardboard boxes	e.g. bottle tops, corks, buttons	
Cardboard tubes	Plastic jar lids	
Clothes-lines x 18m. lengths	Plastic laundry baskets or sledges	
Dried peas, beans, lentils, etc.	Puppets - two - one boy - one girl	
Disposable or plastic cups	Sheet or parachute	

Lesson 1

THE BIRTH OF JOHN THE BAPTIST

Text: Luke 1:5-25,57-66

Teaching Point: John came to prepare the people for the ministry of Jesus.

WARM-UP 1

Everyone stands in a circle holding hands. The leader says, 'I have a message for 'B [specifying a name]' and squeezes either his left or right hand. The recipient squeezes the next person's hand and so on around the circle until 'B' is reached. 'B' calls out, 'Message received.' 'B' decides to send a message to 'C' and the process is repeated. Continue for several turns.

Today's true story from the Bible was about two messengers. Come back and tell me:

1. Who was the first messenger?
2. Who was the second messenger?
3. Why did the second messenger come?

CONSOLIDATION 1

Divide the children into teams. The team members take it in turns to come to the leader, who gives them a strip of paper containing a message to be performed by their teams. Suggested messages are:

1. Lie down on floor with legs and arms in the air for a count of 10 seconds.
2. Form a circle holding hands for a count of 10 seconds.
3. Lie down in a straight line head to foot.
4. Roll from one end of hall to other.
5. Stand on one leg for a count of 10 seconds.

Include sufficient messages to fill up the available time. As soon as a task has been completed a team member returns the message to the leader and is given another one. The first team to complete all the tasks wins.

WIND-UP 1

Remind the children of the warm-up. Was this a good way to send a message? Why not? There was no way of telling what the message was. Refer to the game. Was this a better way to send a message? Go over the answers to the warm-up questions.

THE BIRTH OF JOHN THE BAPTIST

Text: Luke 1:5-25,57-66

Teaching Point: John came to prepare the people for the ministry of Jesus.

WARM-UP 2

A skit or puppets (see script on page 66).

Trudy arrives home from school with exciting news. Her friend, Jemima, has a new baby brother. She tells Toby that the baby has not been given a name, because his parents cannot agree. Everyone in the family thinks this baby is special and his mum thinks he will do something tremendous when he grows up. Toby says the family must be crazy - they think a baby looks like a name and are already planning his future career.

Today's true story from the Bible is about a special baby. Come back and tell me:

1. What was his name?
2. Who chose it?
3. What was he going to do when he grew up?

CONSOLIDATION 2

Divide the children into groups of three. Prepare a set of the following symbols for each group. (See page 87)

- a baby with John underneath
- a wine goblet with a cross through it (no alcohol allowed) (page 83)
- a dove (symbolising the Holy Spirit)
- a group of people (many people)
- a tick (being ready)

Scatter the symbols around the room. The children must link hands to make a line of 3 and find one of each symbol without letting go of each other. Once all the symbols have been collected go through them to see what Gabriel's message was to Zechariah.

Ask the children if Zechariah believed Gabriel's message? What happened as a result? Use a flag to indicate when the children should make a noise or when they should be like Zechariah and unable to speak. Flag up - make a noise, flag down - silence.

WIND-UP 2

Remind the children of the warm-up and go over the answers to the questions. What message did Gabriel bring to Zechariah? Use the game symbols to revise it. Remind the children of the second part of the game. What happened to Zechariah because he did not believe Gabriel's message? What did John come to do? Prepare people for the coming of Jesus.

GOD'S GIFT TO MARY

Text: Luke 1:26-56

Teaching point: Jesus was both man and God.

Lesson 2

WARM-UP 1

Display a selection of boxes, such as cereals, with a list of the contents on the outside. For each one ask the children what is inside the box? How do they know? Read out the list of contents/ ingredients. Open the box to see what is inside. How do they know that the cereal contains all those vitamins? They have to take it on trust.

Today's true story from the Bible is about a person whose mum was given a list of what he would be like. Come back and tell me:

1. Who was the person?
2. What would he be like? [*Son of God, descendant of David, king*]

CONSOLIDATION 1

Label 6 large boxes on the bottom, using one of the following on each: God, Man, King, Prophet, Magician, Doctor. Choose 3 different items to be collected, such as sponges, lids, table tennis balls, etc., and place the same number of each item in each box. The number of items to be collected can be altered according to the amount of time available to play the game, but should be between 2 and 4 of each. If using 2 of each item, each box will contain 6 items, 2 sponges, 2 lids and 2 table tennis balls. Place the 6 boxes around the room.

Divide the children into 3 teams and tell each team which item to collect. Team members take it in turns to run to a box, pick one of their items and return to base. If there are none of their items in the box, the child runs to a different box and picks an item before returning to base. The first team to collect all their items wins.

WIND-UP 1

Remind the children about the warm-up and go over the answers to the questions. Check whether their answers are right by turning over the empty boxes from the game. Ask the children to look at the labels and decide which labels record what Mary was told about Jesus, separating the boxes into 2 groups.

WARM UP 2

A skit or puppets (see script on page 68).

Toby shows Trudy a letter he received at school saying that he has been chosen to represent his county at football. His problem is knowing whether or not to believe it. Trudy points out that the letter looks genuine, his teacher thinks it is genuine and he plays for the school team, so has the ability. If Toby wants to take up the place he must go to training that evening. Trudy encourages Toby to go, but Toby is still not sure that the letter is genuine.

Today's true story from the Bible is about someone who got a message. Come back and tell me:

1. Who sent the message and to whom?
2. What was the message?
3. Did the person believe it?

CONSOLIDATION 2

Responding to a message. Mark off 4-6 areas of the floor that are big enough for all the children to stand on if they squash into a tight group. Mark each area with either a number, a shape or a colour. The children start in the centre of the room. When the leader calls out one of the 4-6 area designators, the children must run to that area and stand on it. Continue, calling out the area designators in random order.

WIND-UP 2

Remind the children about the warm-up and go over the answers to the questions. Did Toby and Trudy believe what Toby was told? How did Mary respond to what she was told by the angel? Link in to the game and the way they responded to the words called out by the leader.

PREPARING PEOPLE FOR THE MESSAGE

Text: Luke 1:66-80; 3:1-18

Teaching Point: John prepares the way for Jesus' coming.

WARM-UP 1

Leader 1 introduces 1 or 2 special guests (other leaders), who are dressed in something weird. Leader 1 asks each guest why he/she is dressed like that, e.g. why are you wearing a turtle on your head? Each guest gives a funny answer, e.g. the turtle keeps the sun off and keeps me cool by waving its arms.

Today's true story from the Bible is about a man who was dressed in strange clothes. Come back and tell me:

1. Who was he?
2. How was he dressed?
3. What was his special job?

CONSOLIDATION 1

Tell the children that they have to prepare for a visit by a king. They must prepare the room by making it clean and tidy. Ask them what else they should do? Include a comfortable chair, nice drink, entertainment. Ask the older children to organise it and give them 10 minutes to prepare. Once the preparations are complete a leader enters wearing a crown and cloak and is greeted by the children, who sit him down and entertain him.

WIND-UP 1

Remind the children of the warm-up and go over the answers to the questions. What was John's special job? To prepare people for the coming of Jesus. Refer to the game. Was this the way John told people to prepare for King Jesus? What did John tell them to do? To repent (say sorry) and be baptised for the forgiveness of sins.

PREPARING PEOPLE FOR THE MESSAGE

Text: Luke 1:66-80; 3:1-18

Teaching Point: John prepares the way for Jesus' coming.

Memory verse: *Believe in the Lord Jesus and you will be saved. Acts 16:31*

Lesson 3

WARM-UP 2

Special clothes for a special job.

Ask for 6 volunteers to dress up in a police helmet, a doctor's stethoscope, a builder's hard hat, a sailor's hat, a soldier's cap, a chef's hat. As each child puts on the clothing ask who they are. Once the correct answer is given turn over the appropriate picture already pinned on the board. (See pages 87 and 91)

How do the children know who does which job? [*the clothes they wear*] In today's true story from the Bible we will find out about a man who had a special job. Come back and tell me:

1. What was his name?
2. What job did he have?
3. What special clothes did he wear?
4. *(for the older children)* Who, in the OT, wore similar clothing? (2 Kings 1)

CONSOLIDATION 2

Divide the children into teams. Prepare one set of 11 memory verse cards for each team by writing one word of the memory verse, including the reference, onto each card. The aim of the game is to collect all the words of the memory verse by completing an obstacle course and giving the password. The obstacle course is designed to remind the children of Isaiah's prophecy concerning what John would do.

Hill - large cushion or chair, valley - small table, rough place - 2 mats or pieces of newspaper, crooked path - masking tape, water of baptism - plastic boat/sledge/box.

The children clamber over the cushion, squirm under the table, squirm over the mats, follow the masking tape (running), jump into the boat and out the other side. On giving the password, '*believe in Jesus,*' to the teacher, the child is given one word of the memory verse to bring back to the start. The child runs back to the start. The next child is sent off as soon as the previous one reaches the teacher at the far end of the course. The winner is the first team to collect the memory verse and put it into the correct order.

WIND-UP 2

Remind the children of the warm-up and go over the answers to the questions. Use the details of the game to remind the children of Isaiah's prophecy regarding John. How did John tell the people to get ready for the coming of Jesus? To repent (say sorry) and be baptised for the forgiveness of sins. Revise the memory verse.

GOD'S GIFT TO THE WORLD

Text: Luke 2:1-20

Teaching Point: Jesus came to save us.

WARM-UP 1

Display 3 or 4 wrapped gifts on a table and say that you got them for Christmas. Point out how beautifully they are wrapped. They must contain something special. You are so excited that you cannot wait for Christmas. Open them one at a time and show the children. Each gift should be something special. After everyone has had a chance to see the great presents, tell the children that the best ever Christmas present did not come in beautiful paper, but in something like this (a disposable nappy).

Today's true story from the Bible is about the best ever Christmas present. Come back and tell me:

1. Why were Mary and Joseph in Bethlehem?
2. What 2 things did the angel tell the shepherds about Jesus? [*Saviour and Lord*]
3. What did the shepherds do after they had seen Jesus?

CONSOLIDATION 1

This consolidation is designed to reinforce that the good news about Jesus is for everyone (v.10). Divide the children into multi-age teams and prepare a set of colour coded cutouts of distinctively shaped islands for each team. Suggested islands are New Zealand, Australia, Madegascar, Cyprus, Sri Lanka, Crete. Pin a map of the world onto a board and hide the cutouts around the room. Give each team a sheet of paper on which are outlines of each island with spaces for the letters of its name underneath. The children find the islands and go to the world map to identify them. Once the island has been identified it is glued onto the sheet of paper and its name is filled in. The winner is the first team to complete the task.

WIND-UP 1

Remind the children of the warm-up and go over the answers to the questions. Refer to the game. Go over the names of the islands and show where they are on the map. Each time ask, 'Did Jesus come for the people of ...?'

GOD'S GIFT TO THE WORLD

Text: Luke 2:1-20

Teaching Point: Jesus came to save us

Memory verse: *God so loved the world that he gave his only Son. John 3:16*

WARM-UP 2

Various leaders bring a wrapped gift for Leader 1. The gifts should be unexpected, such as a physics textbook, or a cabbage. As each gift is proffered Leader 1 expresses surprise at the gift. Leader 1 unwraps the gifts (or asks children to help with the unwrapping) and is even more surprised when he sees what he has been given.

Today's true story from the Bible is about some people who were very surprised to get a gift. Come back and tell me:

1. Who were they?
2. What was the gift?
3. Who told them about the gift?

CONSOLIDATION 2

Divide the children into groups of not more than 12. For each group prepare a parcel wrapped in 13 layers of paper. In the centre of the parcel is a small bag of sweets or similar with a picture of a baby in swaddling clothes stuck to it (see page 85). Place between each layer of wrapping paper a strip of paper containing one word of the memory verse plus reference. These should be in random order. Sit the children in circles facing inwards. Pass the parcel around each circle to music. When the music stops the child holding the parcel removes a layer of wrapping paper and keeps the memory verse strip. The game continues, removing one layer of wrapping paper each time the music stops, until the bag of sweets is unwrapped. Each group places their memory verse strips in verse order, keeping the sweets for later. The winner is the first group to complete the exercise.

WIND-UP 2

Remind the children about the warm-up and go over the answers to the questions. What did the shepherds do after the angel told them about Jesus? Why did God give us such a special gift? Revise the memory verse.

THE BIRTH OF JESUS

Text: Luke 2:1-20

Teaching Point: This baby was truly God.

Memory verse: *Christ Jesus came into the world to save sinners. 1 Timothy 1:15*

WARM-UP 1

Tell the children that you are going on a journey but have not packed your bag. Ask the children to suggest the items you should take. As the children suggest something, see if you have it hidden away and put it into the bag. By the end you have filled your bag with clothes, shower bag, towel, books, shoes, etc. Include some strange items for fun.

Today's true story from the Bible is about some people who went on a journey. Come back and tell me:

1. Who went on the journey?
2. Why were they going on a journey?
3. What special thing happened at the end of the journey?

CONSOLIDATION 1

Divide the children into teams, each one with a leader or older child. Give each team a toilet roll to wrap up their leader to make a swaddled baby. Judge the results.

WIND UP 1

Remind the children of the warm-up and go over the answers to the questions. The special thing that happened at the end of the journey was the birth of a special baby. Refer to the game. Do they think this is what the swaddled baby looked like? How did Jesus differ from any other baby? He was God. How do we know? The angels told the shepherds.

THE BIRTH OF JESUS

Text: Luke 2:1-20

Teaching Point: This baby was truly God.

Memory verse: *Christ Jesus came into the world to save sinners. 1 Timothy 1:15*

WARM-UP 2

Prepare pictures of fathers and sons (see page 89). These should include some easily identifiable ones, such as different nationalities or well-known figures. E.g. an African man and boy, an Indian man and boy, a celebrity and his son, one of the leaders and his son, one or two European men and boys. Pin the pictures of the fathers onto a board. Display the pictures of the sons one by one and ask the children to state whose son he is. Pin each son under the designated father. Once all the sons have been allocated give the children the chance to change their minds regarding who is whose son. Talk about how difficult or easy it was to decide which son belonged to which father. Display the picture of a baby with neutral features. Whose son is he? After the children have finished guessing, point out that there is no way they can know for sure whose son he is just by looking. The only way to find this out is to be told.

Today's true story from the Bible is about a baby boy. Come back and tell me:

1. What was his name?
2. Whose son was he?
3. How do we know whose son he was?

CONSOLIDATION 2

Divide the children into multi-age teams containing no more than 9 players. For each team prepare a set of 9 cards, each of which has a picture on one side and a word of the memory verse on the other. Match up pictures and words as follows: *scroll stating everyone must be counted* / Christ, *Joseph with Mary on a donkey* / Jesus, *sign for The Bethlehem inn* / came, *innkeeper saying, 'No room!'* / into, *Sign 'To the stable'* / the, *a baby* / world, *shepherds* / to, *sheep* / save, *angel* / sinners, *crowd of angels*/ 1 Timothy 1:15. (See pages 83 and 84 for pictures.)

The children start at one end of the room (Nazareth) and take it in turns to race over some obstacles to the other end (Bethlehem), pick up one of their team's pictures and return to base. The first child must return to base before the next child races. Once all the pictures have been collected the children place them in story order. Turn the pictures over to see if the children have got it right. If the pictures are in the correct order the memory verse will be displayed. The winner is the first team to complete the task.

WIND UP 2

Use the pictures from the game to recapitulate the main points of the story. Remind the children of the warm-up and go over the answers to the questions. Point out that we know that Jesus was God's son because God sent the angels to tell the shepherds. Turn the game pictures over to reveal the memory verse. Jesus is only able to save us from the penalty of our sins because he was truly God. Revise the memory verse.

GOOD NEWS PROCLAIMED BY ANGELS

Text: Luke 2:1-20

Teaching Point: Jesus is the Saviour of the world.

Memory verse: *Jesus is the Saviour of the world. John 4:42*

WARM-UP 1

Ask the children if they have ever looked forward to anything? Make a list of events they look forward to, such as Christmas, birthdays, holidays etc. Ask if anyone has heard a town crier announcing special events? Produce a fancy hat (three cornered if possible) and a bell. Put on the hat and show what a town crier does. Ring the bell several times and call out, 'Oyez! Oyez! Oyez! Later there will be drinks and biscuits for everyone.' Ask for volunteers to give a message using the bell and hat.

In today's true story from the Bible someone brings a message. Come back and tell me:

1. Who was the messenger?
2. Who received the message?

3. What was the message?

CONSOLIDATION 1

Divide the children into teams of 8. Prepare a set of memory verse cards for each team by writing a word of the verse and reference, onto each card. The children start at one end of the room and the shuffled cards are placed in piles at the other end. Form an obstacle course. The team members take it in turns to race over the obstacles to the other end of the room, pick up a card and run back to base. The second child runs once the first child has returned. The winner is the first team to collect all their cards and place them in order.

WIND UP 1

Review the warm-up and go over the questions. Refer to the game. How do we know that Jesus is the Saviour of the world? The angels told the shepherds. Revise the memory verse.

WARM-UP 2

Sit down with the children and talk about angels. Ask them what they think angels are like? List their answers on a board. Ask for volunteers to draw angels.

Today's true story from the Bible is about angels. Come back and tell me:

1. To whom did the angels appear?
2. Why?
3. How did the people who saw the angels feel? [*terrified*]

CONSOLIDATION 2

The leaders are the shepherds and the children are sheep. The shepherds chase the sheep. When a sheep is tagged he/she must go to the sheepfold. Whilst the game is in progress a leader calls out periodically, 'Angel!' at which point everyone freezes looking terrified. When the leader calls out, 'Don't be afraid!' the game continues and all the penned sheep are released to rejoin the game. At the end of the game gather all the sheep into the sheepfold for the wind-up.

WIND UP 2

Remind the children about the warm-up and go over the answers to the questions. Link in to the game and their response to the word, 'Angel!' Talk about the good news that the angel brought. What did the shepherds do about it? They went to see the baby and then they told everyone about it.

Lesson 6

GOD'S GIFT TO SIMEON

Text: Luke 2:21-40

Teaching Point: Jesus is the promised Messiah.

WARM-UP 1

Prepare a parcel wrapped in layers of Christmas paper for 'Pass the Parcel'. In each layer place a Christmas picture, some secular and 3 to do with the Bible story - a baby, a pair of doves and a candle (see pictures on page 85). The non-story pictures can be Christmas cards. Talk about Christmas presents. Sit the children in a circle and pass the parcel round to music. When the music stops the child holding the parcel removes one layer of paper and holds up the picture. The children decide whether or not the picture is to do with the Bible story. Pin the pictures to do with the Bible story on one side of the board and the other ones on the other side. Once all the pictures are pinned up allow the children the opportunity to change their minds.

Today's true story from the Bible is to do with some of these things. Come back and tell me which ones are to do with the story and why.

CONSOLIDATION 1

Divide the children into teams. Prepare a number of covered containers (could be envelopes), at least one per child, by placing one of the warm-up pictures (or similar) inside each one. Place the containers in the centre of the room and space the teams equidistant from the centre. Team members take it in turns to run to the containers, pick up one and return to base. If the container has a story symbol inside it is kept, if not it is returned to the centre with the next runner. After a set period of time call the game to a halt and count up the number of story symbols collected by each team. The team with the most symbols wins.

WIND-UP 1

Remind the children of the warm-up and go over the pictures to see if they are in the right place. Talk about Jesus being the light and what this means for us. Thank God for sending Jesus to be our Saviour.

GOD'S GIFT TO SIMEON

Text: Luke 2:21-40

Teaching Point: Jesus is the promised Messiah.

WARM-UP 2

Prepare a series of 6-8 questions and answers on separate strips of card. The questions should be about the leaders.

Suggestions for types of questions:

1. Who is the cleverest leader?
2. Who is the prettiest leader?
3. Who is the tallest leader?
4. Which leader has the most sisters/ brothers?
5. Which leader likes carrots more than peas?
6. Which leader prefers reading a book to going to the cinema?
7. Which leader went to Spain for their holiday?

Pin up the questions one at a time and ask the children to think about the answers they might give. Pin up the answers against the wrong questions, e.g. the answer to question 6 against question 3. Ask the children if they are the answers they expected. Change the answers round so that they are correct. Once again ask the children if those are the answers they expected.

In today's true story from the Bible someone finally gets something he has been expecting. Come back and tell me:

1. Who was he?
2. What was he expecting?

CONSOLIDATION 2

Child 1 goes out of the room and one of the remaining children is given something small to hold or a squeaky toy (or similar) to hide on his/ her person. Child 1 returns and has to decide which child is the chosen one. Child 1 can ask the children to jump up and down, turn round, etc. Child 1 points to a child. If that child is not the chosen one he/she sits down and the game continues until the chosen one is discovered. When the chosen one is discovered another child goes out and a different child becomes the chosen one.

WIND-UP 2

Remind the children about the warm-up and go over the answers to the questions. How did Simeon know that Jesus was the promised Messiah? The Holy Spirit told him. Not like the game where they discovered the chosen one by trial and error.

JESUS PRESENTED AT THE TEMPLE

Text: Luke 2:21-40

Teaching Point: Jesus is the promised Saviour.

Memory verse: *Christ Jesus came into the world to save sinners. 1 Timothy 1:15*

WARM-UP 1

Place various objects in turn on the OHP and ask the children to identify them. As an alternative you could use pictures of objects, people or places. Point out that sometimes it is easy to recognise things and sometimes not. Could they recognise something they had never seen?

In today's true story from the Bible some people recognise someone else they have never seen. Come back and tell me:

1. Who were the people? [*Simeon and Anna*]
2. Whom did they recognise?
3. How did they recognise him?

CONSOLIDATION 1

Divide the children into teams for an obstacle race. The teams start at 'Home' and race to 'The Temple'. Place 2 or 3 obstacles along the course for the children to negotiate. The team members take it in turns to be blindfolded and directed along the course by their team mates. The winner is the first team to get all their players from home to the temple.

This game can be played without blindfolds, but the wind-up will need to be altered accordingly.

WIND-UP 1

The wind-up takes place in the temple. Remind the children about the warm-up and go over the answers. How did Simeon recognise Jesus as the promised saviour? The Holy Spirit told him. Refer to the game and how the children needed direction to negotiate the course from home to the temple. They listened to the voice of someone else. Simeon listened to the Holy Spirit.

WARM-UP 2

Prior to the session place 12 plastic cups upside down on a table and number them from 1-12 on the outside. Hide 4-5 different items, such as a dried pea, lego brick, etc. under the cups, one item per cup.

Tell the children that you have hidden a dried pea under one of the cups and you want them to find it. The children take it in turns to guess the number of cup containing the dried pea. Each time show them what is under the cup before putting it back on the table. If they find the designated item quickly, ask them to find one of the other items.

In today's true story from the Bible someone was looking for someone else he had never seen before. He did not have to guess, like looking for the dried pea. Come back and tell me:

1. What was his name?
2. Who was he looking for?
3. How did he know he had found him?

CONSOLIDATION 2

Prepare 4 sets of memory verse cards by writing one word of the memory verse, including the reference, onto A4 or A5 pieces of paper (40 words in total). Hide the words around the room. Place 10 boxes similar in size at scattered locations through the room. Allocate one older child or leader to each box and give them glue and/or sticky tape. Tell the box keepers which word of the memory verse is for their box. The other children act as finders. When a word is found the child finds the appropriate box and gives the word to the boxkeeper, who fixes it to one side of the box. Once each box has 4 words stuck round its sides the boxes are made into a pillar with the memory verse words reading in order from top to bottom. Add a card flame to the top of the top box to make a candle.

WIND-UP 2

Remind the children about the warm-up and go over the answers to the questions. How did Simeon recognise Jesus as the promised saviour? The Holy Spirit told him. What did Simeon say Jesus would be for the Gentiles? A light. Point to the candle pillar in the centre of the room. Make sure the children know who the Gentiles are. Why did Jesus come? To be our saviour. Revise the memory verse.

JESUS CALLS THE FIRST DISCIPLES

Text: Luke 5:1-11

Teaching Point: Jesus requires his followers to put him first.

WARM-UP 1

Ask the children and leaders to form a line behind Leader 1. They must follow Leader 1 and do what he does. Leader 1 leads the line around the room, sometimes taking slow, giant strides, sometimes with arms outstretched to the sides, sometimes crawling, sometimes hopping.

Today's true story from the Bible is about some men who had to decide whom to follow. Come back and tell me:

1. Who were the men?
2. Who did they follow?
3. What job did they leave behind?

CONSOLIDATION 1

Divide the children into teams and give each team a large container. Place a variety of items in a large pile equidistant from the teams. Team members take it in turns to run to the pile, pick up an item, return to base and place the item in the container. Periodocally the leader changes the number of items individuals can collect from one to two, to three, etc. Continue until all the items have been collected, by which time each team's container should be overflowing. Count up the number of items each team has placed in its container. Items on the floor are not counted. The winner is the team that has collected the most items.

WIND-UP 1

Remind the children of the warm-up and go over the answers to the questions. Talk about the game and what happened when their containers overflowed. What did that remind them of? The disciples with their nets overflowing. Who did the fishermen follow? Jesus called Peter and the others to put him first and he calls us to do the same.

WARM-UP 2

Place a large box on a table in clear view of the children and take out the following items one at a time: a tractor, a farmer, a fisherman, a boat, nets, fish, an elephant, flies, a television, a taxi, a sheep, a clock, a tennis raquet, a book. (See pages 90-92) The items can be real, toys or pictures and can be taken out in any order. Once all have been displayed ask the children to choose 4 that they think might be in the Bible story. Do they know a story about a farmer, a sheep, an elephant and a tennis raquet? Once they have made their selection replace the remaining items in the box.

Today's true story from the Bible is about 4 of the items that you looked at. Come back and see if you chose the right four.

CONSOLIDATION 2

Prior to the lesson cut out 50-60 paper fish about A5 size and place in a box. Divide the children into teams and give each team a tray or glossy magazine on which to carry the fish. The children start at one end of the room and a leader stands with the box of fish at the other. Team members take it in turns to run to the other end of the room with their tray, pick up 1 fish and run back to base with the fish on the tray. They must not touch the fish whilst in transit unless it falls off the tray, at which point they are allowed to stop, pick up the fish and replace it on the tray. Continue for a set period of time. At the end of the game count up the number of fish each team has caught.

WIND-UP 2

Go over the items from the warm-up and see if the children chose correctly. Ask the children to state what the item had to do with the story. Refer to the game and remind the children that Peter, Andrew, James and John were fishermen. What did Jesus call them to do? Jesus called them to follow him and put him first. Jesus calls us to do the same.

SIMON AND THE WOMAN

Text: Luke 7:36-50

Teaching Point: We all need forgiveness and Jesus is willing to forgive us.

Lesson 10

WARM-UP 1

Ask the children if any of them have ever borrowed anything? Discuss length of time things borrowed and what happened when they were due to be given back. Explain that 2 people in the room have borrowed something from you and it is time it was given back. Hand out envelopes to 2 leaders/children and ask them to open them and read them out. (The leaders or children need to be warned in advance.) The first person reads out a statement owing the leader £1.00, which is due to be paid back by the end of the session. The second person owes £1000. Both state that they are unable to pay. The leader reiterates that the debts are due to be repaid by the end of the session.

Today's true story from the Bible is one Jesus told about 2 people who owed money. Come back and tell me:

1. To whom did Jesus tell the story?
2. What happened to the men who owed money?
3. Why did Jesus tell the story?

CONSOLIDATION 1

Play a game of tag with one or more leaders acting as 'It'. This can be done either with the children being chased around the room or running from one end to the other with 'It' standing in the middle. Any child who is tagged must go to Leader 1 and ask, 'Please forgive me?' at which point a sticky dot is attached to their clothing and they rejoin the game.

WIND-UP 1

Remind the children of the warm-up and ask the 2 leaders/children with the debts whether they are able to repay the money? Both answer in the negative. Go over the answers to the questions from the warm-up. Ask the children what should happen to the 2 leaders/children who owe you money? Refer to the game and see which child has the greatest number of sticky dots. Who is the most grateful for forgiveness? The one who needed it most.

WARM-UP 2

Skit or puppets (see page70). Trudy tells Toby that Dad wants to see him immediately, because he found the chocolate box half empty and knows that Toby has eaten them. Toby points out that Trudy had one too. Trudy says it does not matter, because she only took one, whereas Toby had 10. Toby goes off to say sorry to Dad leaving Trudy gloating over his possible punishment. Toby returns to say that Dad has forgiven him and Trudy ought to own up too. Trudy says she does not need to say sorry and flounces off. Ask the children if Trudy needs to be forgiven? Today's true story from the Bible will help you to work out the answer. Listen carefully and come back and tell me whether Trudy needs to say sorry too.

CONSOLIDATION 2

Show the children a jar with something precious in it and place it to one side. Tell them it is very precious to you and no one is to touch it. Play a game such as an obstacle race or parachute game. Whilst the game is in progress a leader removes the jar. At the end of the game discover that the jar is missing. Send the children off to find it. When the children cannot find it bring them back together and comment on how naughty the person is who took the jar. The leader who took the jar comes forward, returns the jar and asks for forgiveness.

WIND-UP 2

Ask the children what should happen to the leader who took the jar? Should he/she be forgiven? Why? Remind the children of the warm-up. Did Trudy need to be forgiven also? Point out that we all need to be forgiven by God because we have all done naughty things. Can anyone be too naughty for God to forgive them? What do we need to do if we want God to forgive us? Be truly sorry and ask him to do so. We show how thankful we are and how much we love God by doing the things that please him.

AUTHORITY OVER DEMONS

Text: Luke 8:26-39

Teaching Point: Jesus has power over demons because he is God.

WARM-UP 1

Ask for volunteers to demonstrate how powerful they are by lifting heavy weights. Start with relatively light weights, such as a chair, a small table, a stack of books. Progress to heavier weights, such as bags containing heavy books or tins. End with virtually impossible items, such as lifting a big table so that all 4 legs are off the ground or a chair with one hand. Make sure that no child or leader attempts to lift in a way that will damage their back. (The table can be lifted up by lying underneath it and planting the feet on the middle of the underside, then pushing up with the legs.) As children fail to complete a task they are eliminated.

Today's true story from the Bible is about someone who was very powerful, but in a different way. Come back and tell me:

1. Who was powerful?
2. How did he show his power?
3. Why was he so powerful?

CONSOLIDATION 1

The Change game. Designate 4 locations to be safe places. Tell the children that they are pigs. They start at one location and, on the order, 'Change', they run on all fours squealing like pigs to any other location. The last child to arrive at each location is out and goes to the sin bin. Continue until only a few children left. If wished, the game can be played by making children who are out miss 2 turns before they rejoin the game.

WIND-UP 1

Remind the children of the warm-up and go over the answers to the questions. Jesus had much greater power than a physically strong man; he had the power to tell demons to flee. Refer to the game and how they changed from place to place. How did Jesus change the demon-possessed man? Why could Jesus do this? Because he is God.

WARM-UP 2

Place a large box on a table in clear view of the audience. Bring out a selection of items one by one, each time asking, 'Do you think this is mentioned in today's true story from the Bible?' Separate the items into 2 groups, depending on the choice made. The items can be real, pictures, models, etc. and suggestions are: a chain, a padlock, a giraffe, a boat, a sheep, a cow, a pig, clothing, bread, fish, weights, a shepherd, a torch. Once all the items have been displayed give the children an opportunity to change their minds.

Today's true story from the Bible is about some of these items. Come back and see if you have chosen correctly.

CONSOLIDATION 2

Divide the children into teams, each with a leader or older child. Place the following items of clothing at 6 different locations: hats, coats, dresses, jumpers, trousers, gloves. You need the same number of each item as there are teams. The children collect clothes from each location and return to base where they dress a leader or older child with the articles of clothing recovered. Award points for the first to be dressed and for the way the leaders have been dressed.

WIND-UP 2

Remind the children of the warm-up and go over the items chosen to see if they were in the story. Use this to revise the story details. What happened to the man once Jesus had healed him? The people from the nearby town found him dressed and in his right mind. Do the children think that the man would have been dressed in the sort of clothes used in the game? Why could Jesus heal the demon-possessed man? Because he is God.

THE TRANSFIGURATION

Text: Luke 9:28-36

Teaching Point: Jesus is God's son and we should listen to him.

WARM-UP 1

Display a selection of noise making items. Demonstrate the noise made by each item. Place a screen between the leader and the children. The leader picks an item and makes a noise. The children have to listen carefully and shout out the item used. Continue for 2-3 minutes, picking the items at random.

Today's true story from the Bible is about some people who were told to listen. Come back and tell me:

1. What were their names?
2. Who told them to listen?
3. Who should they listen to and why?

CONSOLIDATION 1

Prepare 7 identical containers with lids, 3 empty and 4 containing a cardboard cutout of an ear with a coin sellotaped to the back. The children hunt for the boxes, but when they hear one of the following sounds they must obey the associated command.

- trumpet - fall flat on the floor
- bell - come out fighting like a boxer/ dance around
- hammer/gavel - jump up and down on the spot
- whistle - do 10 bunny hops (or similar)

Anyone who fails to obey the sound has a sticky dot attached to their clothing. When a box is found the finder calls out, 'Found!' and everyone stops where they are. A leader shakes the box and asks the children to guess what is in it. Once all the boxes have been found they are opened to see what they contain. (If time permits the boxes can be rehidden and the game continue. Do not open the boxes until the end of the game.) The winners are those children without sticky dots.

This game can be played as individuals or in teams.

WIND-UP 1

Remind the children of the warm-up and go over the answers to the questions. Refer to the game and the importance of listening for the various sounds so that they could do what was required. What happened to those children who failed to listen properly? They got a minus point (sticky dot). Why did some of the game boxes contain ears? To remind us of the importance of listening to Jesus. Why must we listen to Jesus? Because he is God's Son. How do we listen to Jesus? Through the Bible.

THE TRANSFIGURATION

Text: Luke 9:28-36

Teaching Point: Jesus is God's son and we should listen to him.

WARM-UP 2

Two leaders are in conversation. Leader 1 says that he has just seen 2 people who have been dead for ages. Leader 2 asks who? Leader 1 names 2 people from history, e.g. Henry VIII and Anne Boleyn, Sir Walter Raleigh and Queen Elizabeth I, Julius Caesar and William the Conqueror. Check that the children know whom is being talked about and explain if necessary. Leader 2 asks where Leader 1 saw them, how he knew who they were and what they were doing. Leader 1 answers the questions as they are asked, ending with the 2 historical characters having a conversation. Leader 2 says Leader 1 must be crazy, because dead people do not come back to life.

Leader 1 concludes with, 'In today's true story from the Bible we will learn about Jesus talking to some people who had been dead for a long, long time. Come back and tell me:

1. Who were they?
2. What were they talking about?
3. Who was listening?

CONSOLIDATION 2

Tell the children to listen very carefully because you will speak quietly. The children mill around in the centre of the room. When a number is called the children must form groups of that number. Any children left over must go to Leader 2, who tells them quietly to go back and rejoin the game. Repeat as time allows. Sometimes, instead of calling a number, ask a question requiring a number answer, e.g. 'How many disciples went up the mountain with Jesus? (3) How many people came from heaven to talk to Jesus? (2) How many people were on the mountain in total? (6)

WIND-UP 2

Remind the children of the warm-up and go over the answers to the questions. Refer to the game and the importance of listening for the numbers so that they could do what was required. Why did we play a listening game? To remind us of the importance of listening to Jesus. Why must we listen to Jesus? Because he is God's Son. How do we listen to Jesus? Through the Bible.

THE GOOD SAMARITAN

Text: Luke 10:25-37

Teaching Point: The way we behave should demonstrate that we belong to God.

WARM-UP 1

Leader 1 talks to the children about a favourite holiday, book, TV show or pet. Leader 2 is hiding nearby and, at the appropriate time, quietly calls out, 'Help!' Leader 2 gradually increases the volume until the children hear the sound or go looking for the source of the cry. Leader 1 prompts the group by saying, 'Quiet! Did you hear anything?' Even when the cry for help is clearly audible, Leader 1 tells the children to ignore it. The children will probably insist on trying to help the person. If the children ignore the cry for help Leader 1 asks them why they chose to do nothing. If they respond to the cry he asks them why they decided to. Finally, Leader 1 rescues the person in trouble.

Today's true story from the Bible is one Jesus told about someone who needed help. Come back and tell me:

1. Who needed help and why?
2. Who gave the help?
3. Why was this surprising?

CONSOLIDATION 1

The children must find their partner (neighbour) and the older child must help the younger one achieve a task, such as hopping the length of the room. Prepare a collection of tokens, one per child, with the tokens marked so that pairs can be identified. (Tokens could be table tennis balls.) Place the marked tokens in a container.

Explain what the children must do and empty the container so that the tokens spill on the floor. The children pick one and find their neighbour. Once everyone has found their neighbour have a race with the older child helping the younger.

WIND-UP 1

Remind the children of the warm-up and go over the answers. Point out that the 2 people who would be expected to help the man were the priest and Levite, not the Samaritan. Refer to the game. Which one of the pair was the helper? The older one. Was this what they would expect? Reinforce the fact that the Samaritan was the one who acted like a neighbour, not the religious people. We show Jesus how much we love him by treating other people in the right way.

WARM-UP 2

Perform the script on page 72 with a puppet. The puppet squeaks or nods after each statement by the leader. Leader asks the children if Jemima behaved like a real friend? Today's true story from the Bible is about how Jesus expects us to behave to other people. Come back and tell me:

1. Who needed a friend and why?
2. Which person acted like a friend?
3. Why was this surprising?

CONSOLIDATION 2

The children move around the room to music. When the music stops the leader calls out a number, at which point the children form groups of that number, holding hands. Each time they must be holding different people's hands. No-one is out. Repeat as time allows. The final number called is the total number of children present, so that one big group is formed.

WIND-UP 2

Remind the children of the warm-up and go over the answers. Refer to the game. Who was in the final group? Everyone. Who is my neighbour? Everyone. To whom must we do good? Everyone.

MARY AND MARTHA

Text: Luke 10:38-42

Teaching Point: We need to spend time listening to Jesus.

WARM-UP 1

Leader 1 reads a story to the children. Whilst this is happening Leader 2 starts tidying up the area, making a noise and generally getting in the way. Leader 1 repeatedly asks Leader 2 to be quieter, etc. Finally Leader 2 dusts Leader 1 with a feather duster. Leader 1 becomes very irritated and shouts at Leader 2 to go away. One of the leaders points out that both leaders were trying to do different things and getting in each other's way. Neither leader behaved very well.

In today's true story from the Bible 2 ladies are wanting to do different things. Come back and tell me:

1. What were their names?
2. What did each one want to do?
3. What did Jesus say about it?

CONSOLIDATION 1

Designate several areas as rooms in a house, e.g. a dining area, a kitchen and a lounge area and place appropriate props haphazardly in each area. Allocate groups of children to each area, each group under the leadership of an older child. On the command, 'Martha!' the children tidy their area as quickly as possible. On the command, 'Mary!' the children assemble around a leader, who reads Luke 10:41-42 to them. Whilst the Bible passage is being read, other leaders mess up the areas. Allocate children to a different area and repeat the process. Progress to the wind-up after the last reading of the Bible passage.

WIND-UP 1

Remind the children of the warm-up and go over the answers to the questions. Refer to the game. Who did Jesus say chose the better thing - Martha or Mary? Reinforce the importance of spending time listening to Jesus by hearing or reading Bible stories.

WARM-UP 2

Leader 1 is very busy getting the area ready for the session. He tells the children that he was late arriving and needs help to get ready. Whilst the area is being readied Leader 1 is continually muttering to himself about getting it right, running out of time, etc. He keeps correcting what the children have done to help to make it 'right'. Leader 2 points out that it is time to go for the Bible story. Leader 1 says that he still has a lot of work to do, so cannot possibly go for the Bible story. Leader 2 sends the children off.

Today's true story from the Bible is about 2 ladies. Come back and tell me:

1. Which one was too busy?
2. Which one listened?
3. What did Jesus say about it?

CONSOLIDATION 2

Sit the children in a circle facing inwards. One child is 'It'. 'It' walks around the circle behind the children and touches one on the back. The child who is touched must get up quickly and chase 'It' around the circle. If 'It' can run round the circle and sit in the chasing child's place before being tagged the chasing child becomes 'It'. If 'It' is tagged before reaching the spare place in the circle the chasing child resumes his/her place and 'It' continues to walk around the circle and chooses a different child.

WIND-UP 2

Remind the children about the warm-up and go over the answers to the questions. Refer to the game. How did 'It' choose someone? In the story, who did Jesus say chose the better thing? Mary.

THE CRIPPLED WOMAN

Text: Luke 13:10-17

Teaching Point: God is more concerned about people's needs than about religious rules.

WARM-UP 1

Show the children an item that has been broken and ask for volunteers to try and mend it. Provide sticky tape, string, paper and rubber bands.

Today's true story from the Bible is about a woman who was damaged. Come back and tell me:

1. How did Jesus make her better?
2. Why did this make some people angry?

CONSOLIDATION 1

Place a large number of items, such as small cushions, cardboard boxes, plastic ice-cream containers, biscuit tins, etc., in a pile in the centre of the room. Designate a shape, such as circle, square, or triangle. On the command, 'Immediately!' the children must arrange the items into the designated shape, with each item touching the one either side of it. See how long it takes to complete the exercise and tell the children the time. Repeat a couple of times, giving a different shape, to see which one is completed the fastest.

This could be played as a team game.

WIND-UP 1

Remind the children of the warm-up and how difficult it was to repair the item. Could they do it immediately? Go over the answers to the wind-up questions. Refer to the game. Were they able to make the required shape immediately? Jesus was able to heal the lady immediately because he is God.

THE CRIPPLED WOMAN

Text: Luke 13:10-17

Teaching Point: God is more concerned about people's needs than about religious rules.

WARM-UP 2

Leader 2 enters dressed up to go somewhere special. Leader 2 is in great distress and tells Leader 1 that she has just had an accident. Her car has collided with a cyclist. She tells Leader 1 how distressed she is because her make-up is ruined, her hair is in a mess, her car is scratched and, worst of all, she is late for church. Leader 1 asks Leader 2 if the cyclist is alright. Leader 2 does not know - she did not look, because it would have made her even later for church. Leader 1 asks the children what they think about Leader 2's behaviour. Would they like to say anything to her? Point out that Leader 2 has got her priorities wrong. Reassure the children that there was no accident, it was just a bit of make believe.

In today's true story from the Bible there are some people who are just like this woman and care about the wrong things. Come back and tell me:

1. Who were they?
2. What did they care about?
3. What should they have cared about?

CONSOLIDATION 2

Divide the children into groups of 5-7 and give each group a die and pieces of card to make the crippled woman (see page 86). Each group needs a flat surface and bluetak so the pieces can be stuck on to make the woman. The children take it in turns to throw the die. A six must be thrown first to get the upper body, followed by a five for the skirt. Following that the children must throw a four for the head, 2 threes for the legs and 1 two for the left arm. These can be thrown in any order. The final throw is for the right arm with the stick. The first team to complete the exercise wins. Once the crippled woman has been made, repeat the exercise, this time making the woman standing upright (healed).

WIND-UP 2

Remind the children of the warm-up and go over the answers to the questions. Refer to the game. Who made the woman better? Jesus. Point out that Jesus was more concerned about the woman's need of healing than about keeping religious rules.

THE GREAT FEAST

Text: Luke 14:15-24

Teaching Point: Those who reject God's invitation will in the end be rejected by God.

WARM-UP 1

Prior to the lesson write the following list onto a flipchart, board or OHP:

- Birthday cake
- Birthday card
- Birthday present
- Birthday treat
- Birthday surprise
- Birthday suit

Cover each of the words following 'Birthday' with a strip of card. Starting with the top phrase, ask the children to guess what word is underneath the card. Reveal the first letter of the word if they get stuck. Once all the words are revealed ask what is missing, i.e. Birthday party. Ask the children what other parties they have been to apart from birthday ones.

In today's true story from the Bible we will hear a story Jesus told about a man who gave a great big party. Come back and tell me:

1. Who came to the party?
2. What excuses did people give for not coming?
3. Why did Jesus tell this story?

Prepare party invitations in advance and hand one out to each child. The children go to Bible time and give their invitation to the leader for safekeeping.

CONSOLIDATION 1

Only those who return with their invitations will be allowed into the consolidation.

Designate 4 locations with 'doorways' marked by chairs. Mark each location with a colour or symbol. At each location place 2 large boxes, 1 empty and 1 full of some easily transportable object such as table tennis balls, lids, sponge balls, sponges, etc.

The children start in the centre. When the colour of the location is called (red, blue, yellow, green) the children race to the party carrying their invitation, enter the door, drop the invitation in the empty container and pick up a new invitation from the full container (i.e. one of the items), returning to the middle. Anyone without an invitation is out. Continue for several turns, terminating with the written invitation.

WIND-UP 1

Remind the children about the warm-up and go over the answers to the questions. Refer to the game. What happened to those people who failed to present an invitation, either at the beginning of the game or after each round? They were not allowed to take any further part. In the story Jesus told, what happened to those people who refused to come to the party? God loves us and wants us to be at his party in heaven. We need to say thank you for his invitation.

THE GREAT FEAST

Text: Luke 14:15-24

Teaching Point: Those who reject God's invitation will in the end be rejected by God.

WARM-UP 2

Place a pile of items on a table in clear view of the children. Items can include clothing, toys, pictures and fruit. Hold up the items one by one and ask the children whether it should be accepted or rejected. Clothing might be dirty, smelly, the wrong colour or style. Toys might be broken, fruit might be bad and pictures might be crumpled or torn. Place the acceptable items in one pile and the rejected items in another pile. Point out that you rejected items for a variety of reasons.

In today's true story from the Bible some people were rejected. Come back and tell me:

1. Who rejected them?
2. Why were they rejected?

CONSOLIDATION 2

Provide everything necessary to set up for a party, e.g. plates, cups, tablecloths, bowls of crisps, biscuits, fruit drink, etc. The children set up tables and chairs and lay the tables ready for a party. There must be enough places for all the children and the leaders. If there are a large number of children some of them could make place names. When everything is ready the children invite the leaders to come to the party. The leaders make excuses. The children sit down and enjoy the party. Part way through the leaders change their minds. Ask the children what happened in the Bible story? When the people changed their minds were they allowed into the party? The leaders are refused entry to the party.

WIND-UP 2

Remind the children of the warm-up and go over the answers to the questions. Refer to the game and how disappointed the leaders were at not being allowed into the party. God loves us and wants us to be at his party in heaven. We need to say thank you for his invitation and not be like those people who ended up being shut out.

THE LOST SHEEP

Text: Luke 15:1-7

Teaching Point: Jesus came to save sinners (us).

WARM-UP 1

Prepare 10 piles of coco pops, 9 piles of 10 and 1 pile of 9. Write on a board or flip chart a recipe for a crispy crackle, e.g. 25g butter, 1 tbs golden syrup, 25g chocolate powder, 100 coco pops. Before the children arrive hide a coco pop in the room. Tell the children that you are going to make a crispy crackle and ask them to read out the ingredients so that you can check that you have everything. Put out each item as it is called out. Count out the coco pops on the OHP so the children can see how many are there. Discover one is missing. You can't continue until it is found. The children search until the missing coco pop is found. Always have a spare one in your pocket in case the hidden coco pop gets stepped on.

Today's true story from the Bible is about something that was missing. Come back and tell me:

1. What was missing?
2. Who found it?
3. Why did Jesus tell this story?

CONSOLIDATION 1

Hide a toy sheep (or a paper cut-out, see page 91). The children go out of the room, or are penned in, while it is hidden. While this happens they count to 99. When the sheep is found everyone cheers loudly. The finder is presented with a 'sheep finder' rosette made from ribbon or card. Point out how important it was to find the sheep. Everyone claps the sheep finder.

WIND-UP 1

Remind the children of the warm-up and go over the answers to the questions. Show a bigger, more fancy rosette than the one awarded to the sheep finder. Explain that this is a 'people finder' rosette. Who is the people finder? Jesus. Talk about how much bigger and more important is the task of saving people. Jesus came to save lost people. How do we help in this? By telling our friends about him.

WARM-UP 2

Before the children arrive, hide a table tennis ball or small object, such as a bead or marble, somewhere in the room. Place a box of 99 of the same objects near the edge of a table. Accidentally knock the box off the table. Ask the children to help pick them up. Count them out to discover that there are only 99 there. Tell the children that you need 100 objects for the game. Ask them to search for the missing object.

Today's true story from the Bible is about something that was missing. Come back and tell me:

1. What was missing?
2. Who found it?
3. Why did Jesus tell this story?

CONSOLIDATION 2

Construct 2 sheepfolds from any available equipment, such as tables, chairs, partitions, etc. Designate 2 older children to be shepherds. The remaining children are sheep and can only crawl. (For a large group of children you need 1 sheepfold + a shepherd for approximately 12 children.) The sheep hide whilst the shepherds count to 99. The sheep can baa to identify themselves. The shepherds search for their sheep. When a sheep is found it is led back to the sheepfold. If the shepherd leaves the sheep before it is penned in the sheepfold the sheep can run off and hide again. When all the sheep have been found they are counted to see which shepherd found the most sheep.

A leader should be allocated to each sheepfold to amuse the sheep who have been caught.

WIND-UP 2

Remind the children of the warm-up and go over the questions. Refer to the game and the importance of finding the sheep. Talk about how much bigger and more important is the task of finding people. Jesus came to save lost people. How do we help in this? By telling our friends about him.

THE LOST COIN

Text: Luke 15:8-10

Teaching Point: We are precious to God and he wants us to belong to him.

WARM-UP 1

Show the children a collection of coins. Ask the children what they are and which are the most precious? Work out what you can buy with each coin. Show some foreign coins and how they differ from the first ones. Pick up a coin with a milled edge, such as a £1 coin, and tell the children that it is really precious because you can use it to analyse someone's character. Choose a leader to help you demonstrate. You need the coin, a soft lead pencil and a piece of paper divided into 9 squares. Tell the volunteer to close their eyes, roll the edge of the coin across their face and slap it down on the paper. Draw round the coin, making sure that you get plenty of pencil lead on the edge of the coin. The volunteer repeats the exercise a further 4 times so that there are 5 coin shapes on the paper. By this time there should be 4 black streaks on the volunteer's face. Tell the volunteer that you know they are gullible!

Today's true story from the Bible is one Jesus told about some coins. Come back and tell me:

1. How many coins were in the story?
2. Were the coins precious or ordinary?
3. Why did Jesus tell this story?

CONSOLIDATION 1

Divide the children into teams. The team members take it in turns to race to the other end of the room, pick up a coin, such 2p, place it on their head and walk back to their team without dropping the coin. The coin must not be touched whilst it is on the head. Each team collects 9 coins in this way, then searches the room to find a tenth coin. The winner is the first team to collect ten coins.

WIND-UP 1

Remind the children of the warm-up and go over the answers to the questions. How do we know that the coins were precious? Because the woman searched until she found the lost one. Refer to the game and the need to search for the final coin if they wanted to win. Point out that they are precious to Jesus - he cared enough to die for them.

WARM-UP 2

Write down on small pieces of paper reasons why the children are precious to God or evidence for them being precious. Stick these face down around the walls. Choose children to come out and take one piece of paper off the wall. The child brings the paper to the leader, who reads out why they are precious.

Today's true story from the Bible is one Jesus told about something that was precious. Come back and tell me:

1. What was precious?
2. Why did Jesus tell the story?

CONSOLIDATION 2

Divide the children into teams for a relay race. Split the teams so that half of each team is at one end of the room and half at the other end. Each team needs a broom and a silver coin (ball of kitchen foil). The first player sweeps the 'coin' to the other end of the room and hands the broom to the next player, who sweeps it back to the other end. Continue until all have changed places. The first team to finish wins. If time allows repeat the game adding in extra 'coins' to be swept from one end of the room to the other, i.e. each child sweeps 2 or 3 'coins' at the same time.

WIND-UP 2

Remind the children of the warm-up and go over the answers to the questions. Refer to the game and the need to sweep carefully to get the 'coin' from one end of the room to the other. The woman swept her whole house to find her missing coin. Use the papers from the warm-up to remind the children that they are precious to God. They are so precious that Jesus died for them, so that they can be friends with God and part of his family.

THE LOST SON

Text: Luke 15:11-32

Teaching Point: God wants to save us; we need to repent.

Lesson 19

WARM-UP 1

Tell the children that you have a list of jobs to do and need their help. Mime each job, asking them to identify it. Once they guess ask them to mime the job. Jobs could be: Clean up the house ; Feed the chickens; Feed the pigs (pig mush); Water the garden (spray bottle-window cleaner bottle). One of these jobs happens in today's true story from the Bible. Come back and tell me which.

CONSOLIDATION 1

Feed the pigs game. You need buckets, table tennis balls, old telephone directory or newspapers to roll up into balls for food.

Divide the children into four groups and designate 4 areas to act as pigsties. Spread the the same amount of food over the floor of each sty. On command, each group picks up food, races to deposit it in another sty and races back to their own to discover what has been deposited in their sty. Continue until all the food has been deposited elsewhere.

The game finishes when the whole team is back in an empty sty. Alternatively, end at a set point in time and the winning team is the one with least amount of food in their sty. Repeat as necessary. The game could be varied, by putting all the food in one location and having the pigs collect it. Whoever collects the most, wins.

WIND-UP 1

Congregate in one of the pigsties. Remind the children of the warm-up and game. Talk about the son and what brought him to his senses. What did he need to do if he wanted to return to his father? Point out that the father was longing for his son to return. Reinforce the lesson aim.

WARM-UP 2

Identify someone to be Mr. Seymour Clearly, who should be dressed as a handy man. He shows the children some broken items that need mending, such as a piece of timber broken in half, a torn book, sheet of paper or picture, a piece of material with a hole in it. Include items that cannot be mended, such as shredded paper, a sliced up banana, etc. Seymour Clearly sets out the broken items and takes out of his toolkit some string, glue, packing tape and sticky tape. He asks for volunteers to help put the broken items back together.

Today's true story from the Bible is not about mending things but about mending relationships. Come back and tell me:

1. Whose relationship needed mending?
2. How was it mended?
3. Why did Jesus tell the story?

CONSOLIDATION 2

The 'Saying Sorry' game. This is a tag game with the aim of the person who is out trying to get back into the game. A leader is 'It'. Any tagged person goes to a designated area and does an activity such as 6 star jumps to get a sorry card. They take the card to a second leader and exchange it for a forgiveness card and then rejoin the game. Continue for 5 minutes then count who has collected the most/fewest.

Alternatively, use a clothesline to make a winding circular course. The children walk along the line without falling off. Any who fall off must collect a sorry card and exchange it for a forgiveness card, as in first game. Extra leaders can try to distract the children so that they fall off the line.

WIND-UP 2

Remind the children of the warm-up and go over the answers to the questions. Refer to the game. Emphasise that we only need to be forgiven once to enter God's family, not multiple times. We are forgiven when we truly say sorry (repent) and believe in what Jesus has done on the cross. There he took my punishment so that I could be friends with God forever. However, we do have to say sorry everyday for continually falling off God's path (breaking God's rules).

TEN LEPERS

Text: Luke 17:11-19

Teaching Point: The need to associate miracles with God's goodness and to be thankful.

WARM-UP 1

Place 10 cut-outs of people (see diagram on this page) all stacked on top of each other to show one clear image on the OHP. Ask the children to identify the shape. Peel them off one at a time and place them on the OHP until all 10 are visible. Remove them from the OHP and place some other objects onto the screen one at a time, each time asking the children to identify the object. Start with easy objects, such as scissors and a pencil, progressing through harder objects, such as a chess piece and a pencil sharpener, to very hard ones, such as a matchstick, battery and lego brick on its side. End with 9 coco pops and one rice crispie. Ask the children to count the number of coco pops/rice crispies. Ask if they can remember how many people were placed on the OHP at the beginning of the warm-up? Tell the children that one of the ten coco pops/ rice crispies is different from the other 9. Can they guess which one?

Today's true story from the Bible is about 10 of something. Come back and tell me:

1. What or who are 10 in number?
2. What happened to the ten?
3. How did one differ from the others?

CONSOLIDATION 1

Divide the children into teams. Hold up an article and ask the children to find 9 others. The first team to find 9 gets a point. The winning team is the first one to amass 10 points.

Suggested articles: small cardboard box, coin, table tennis ball, disposable cup, plastic box, shoe, shoe lace, coat, sock, Bible, craft activity, pencil, crayon.

WIND-UP 1

Remind the children of the warm-up and go over the answers to the questions. Refer to the game. Why did they collect 9 of each item? Why was that number and the number 10 important? What made one of the lepers different from the other nine? Point out that we should recognise God's goodness to us and be thankful. Discuss what sort of things we should thank God for. Finish with some short thank you prayers.

TEN LEPERS

Text: Luke 17:11-19

Teaching Point: The need to associate miracles with God's goodness and to be thankful.

WARM-UP 2

Leaders take it in turns to mime an action that demonstrates an occupation, such as sweeping the floor, digging, cleaning a window, etc. The children guess the action being mimed. Leader 1 asks the children what sort of person might perform that action? They do this, therefore they are a …

Today's true story from the Bible is about Jesus doing something. Come back and tell me:

1. What did Jesus do?
2. What does this mean Jesus is?

CONSOLIDATION 2

Divide the children into teams of not more than 10, each with a leader or older child. Prepare a set of 10 lepers for each team (see diagram on page 84), one of which is a different colour. place a leader at one end of the room with the leper cutouts. The teams start at the opposite end. Give each team leader a set of 10 questions and answers from the Bible passage (see below). On the command to start, the team leaders read out the first question to his/her team. When it is answered correctly a child runs to the leader at the opposite end, says, 'Thank you' and is handed a leper cutout (See page 87). The child runs back to the team and the second question is read out. Continue until all lepers have been collected. The first team to collect 10 lepers wins. The leader handing out the lepers must make sure that each team collects one different coloured leper.

WIND-UP 2

Remind the children about the warm-up. You can tell what someone is by what they do, (refer to the occupations mimed). Go over the answers to the warm-up questions. Jesus did things only God could do, which means that Jesus is God. Refer to the game. How many lepers were collected? Which is the odd one out? The one who said thank you. We need to recognise God's goodness to us and be thankful.

Lesson 20

1. Where was Jesus going?	*Jerusalem*
2. How many lepers met Jesus?	*10*
3. What was a leper?	*Someone with a skin disease.*
4. Why were they outside the village?	*So that other people would not catch the disease.*
5. What did they ask Jesus to do?	*Have pity on them i.e. heal them.*
6. What did Jesus tell the lepers to do?	*Go and show themselves to a priest.*
7. What happened on their way to the priest?	*They were healed.*
8. How many came back to say thank you?	*1*
9. What else did the man do?	*Praised God.*
10. What nationality was the man?	*Samaritan*

PERSEVERANCE IN PRAYER

Text: Luke 18:1-8

Teaching Point: The importance of persisting in prayer, being certain that God will answer.

WARM-UP 1

Percy Verence and his horse named Prayer. Percy introduces himself as a pony express rider. (Improvise clothing as available.) His job is to get the mail through on his trusty horse, Prayer. He will not give up; he will not be discouraged. At the back of the room is a large, very heavy sack of 'letters'. Percy asks for a volunteer to bring the sack to him to see what is inside. The volunteer drags the bag, without help, to the front of the room, all the time being encouraged by Percy. 'Don't be discouraged! Don't give up! Keep going!' Percy opens the bag and takes out 6 cards, each one with one of the following letters on it: P, R, A, Y, E, R. Percy shows them to the children. Birthday cards could be taken out for any children celebrating birthdays.

Today's true story from the Bible is about keeping going in prayer. Come back and tell me:

1. Why did Jesus tell this story?
2. What can we be certain of when we pray?

CONSOLIDATION 1

Divide the children into teams. Each child requires a 'parcel' to deliver. (Parcels could be sponges, envelopes or pieces of card/paper.) On command, the first child from each team races to the other end of the room carrying their 'parcel', touches a marker, races back and places their parcel on the floor at the front of the team. The second child does the same, placing his parcel in front of and touching the previous parcel. Continue until all the children have raced, by which time their parcels should be making a long line in the direction of the marker. Then child 1 picks up the parcel from the back of the line, races down the room, touches the marker, races back and places the parcel at the front of the line. Continue until the line reaches the marker. Whilst this is going on leaders shout encouragement to their teams.

WIND-UP 1

Remind the children of the warm-up and go over the answers to the questions. Discuss what happens when God does not answer straight away? Why should they keep on praying? They know God **will** answer. Refer to the game and the need to keep on going, even when they were tired. Discuss how prayer can be hard work, but God expects us to keep on praying. Talk about how this helps us to grow as Christians.

PERSEVERANCE IN PRAYER

Text: Luke 18:1-8

Teaching Point: The importance of persisting in prayer, being certain that God will answer.

WARM-UP 2

The object of the exercise is to introduce the famous tri-athlete (Mr. Kenny Do-it or Mrs. Sheila Make-it). The tri-athlete has to pretend to swim 5 miles, then ride 20 miles and finally run 10 miles. Place the swimming items at one location, the cycling items at another and the running clothing at a third location. All locations need to be in clear sight of the audience.

The children will be invited to copy the tri-athlete at each discipline. Make each element last for a couple of minutes so that the children feel it getting harder. Start with the swim. Tell the audience that you are getting tired, how are they feeling. Should we give up? Go to the bike and start the ride. Instruct the children to lie on their backs and make a pedal motion with their legs in the air. Continue for a couple of minutes starting fast and slowing up as you get tired. Should we give up? Now the run. Running on the spot. Monitor how the group is going. Look exhausted at the end.

Today's true story from the Bible is about keeping on going when we may want to give up. What is it that we should never give up on and why? Tell me after the story.

CONSOLIDATION 2

Divide the children into 2 teams. The object is see which team gives up first. Encourage both teams as the game unfolds and especially when it gets harder.

Place 2 partitions end to end to form a wall in the middle of the room. Place equal numbers of items on either side of the partition wall. Suggested items are inflated balloons, soft balls, plastic shopping bags filled with balls of newspaper, table tennis balls, sponges, disposable cups. Mark out a square area either side of the partition wall like a tennis court, treating the partition wall as the net.

Each team must clear their area of all items by throwing them over the partition so that they fall within the marked square. Any items falling outside the marked area will be returned to the offending team. To make it more difficult the leader may reduce the numbers in each team as the game progresses. As the numbers are reduced the effort required for those left is severely increased. Will they persevere? Add more helpers as the participants get tired. Encourage both teams to keep going and not to give up. Stop occasionally to see which team has the most items to get rid of.

WIND-UP 2

Remind the children of the warm-up and go over the answer to the question. Refer to the game and the need to keep on going, even when they were tired. Discuss how prayer can be hard work, but God expects us to keep on praying. Talk about how this helps us to grow as Christians. Why should they keep on praying? They know God **will** answer.

HUMILITY IN PRAYER

Text: Luke 18:9-14

Teaching Point: We are able to draw near to God on the basis of what he has done for us, not what we do for him.

WARM-UP 1

Leader 1 boasts to the children how clever he his. He is much cleverer than anyone else. He is especially clever at arithmetic/numbers. Leader 2 interrupts Leader 1 and says, if Leader 1 is so clever he should tell them the answer to 6 x 9. Leader 1 answers, '53.' Leader 2 corrects him, 'No its not, its 54.' Leader 1 says, 'Oh, well, that's near enough!' Continue in the same vein with different leaders asking Leader 1 to do simple sums, which he gets wrong.

Today's true story from the Bible is about a man who thought he was better than everyone else. Come back and tell me:

1. Who was the man?
2. Why did he think he was better than other people?
3. What does God think about people like that?

CONSOLIDATION 1

The children start at one end of the room. The leaders stand in the middle of the room holding sheets stretched between them. On command the children attempt to get past the leaders without being trapped in the sheets. Any children that get past are chased by leaders with a sheet until all the children are trapped. Once all the children are trapped, Leader 1 counts to 5 slowly out loud, during which time children can shout, 'Mercy!' Those shouting, 'Mercy!' are released and the game is replayed. Any children not asking for mercy are out of the game and go to the sin bin.

WIND-UP 1

Remind the children of the warm-up and go over the answers to the questions. Refer to the game and what happened to those children who did not take the opportunity to ask for mercy. We are not made right with God by keeping religious rules, like the Pharisee thought. We need to say sorry to God for all the naughty things we do and ask him to forgive us.

Lesson 22

HUMILITY IN PRAYER

Text: Luke 18:9-14

Teaching Point: We are able to draw near to God on the basis of what he has done for us, not what we do for him.

WARM-UP 2

Show the children pictures of people who provide something, such as doctor, nurse, postman, shopkeeper, teacher. (See pages 90-93) As each picture is shown, ask children to identify the person and say what they do.

Today's true story from the Bible is about something that only God can do for us. Come back and tell me:

1. What is it?
2. How do we get it?

CONSOLIDATION 2

A team race played in multi-age groups. The object is to rescue your team from the island. Divide the group into no more than 3 teams and mark an area at one end of the room to be the island. (The number of teams is dependent on the number of children.) All team members apart from 1 older child are marooned on the island. The older children are placed at the other end of the room with 1 plastic sledge (or laundry basket with cardboard attached to the base), 2 lengths of rope, a ball of string and a sock. The sledges (or laundry baskets) are the rescue boats and are named, Rescue, Mercy and Forgiveness. The older children have to work out how to use their equipment to rescue their team members. They may need prompting. The rescue is performed by attaching 2 lengths of rope to the rope already attached to the sledge (or a length of rope to either end of the laundry basket). Attach the other end of one piece of rope to the ball of string. Place the ball of string in a sock and throw it over to the island. The children on the island pull on the string to bring the end of the rope to the island. Then they pull on the rope to transport the sledge or laundry basket across. The children can be pulled across in turn in the sledge or laundry basket. It is important to keep hold of the rope at both ends.

NB This game is used also for the lesson on Daniel and the Lions in Book 2 Old Testament. Children enjoy playing it, but it should not be used if previously used in the last 4-6 weeks.

WIND-UP 2

Remind the children of the warm-up and go over the answers to the questions. How was the man in the story rescued / made right with God? By asking for forgiveness. Refer to the game. Could the children on the island rescue themselves? They relied on the rescuer to save them. If the rescuer had not thrown the lifeline they would have been stuck on the island. We cannot rescue ourselves. We need to go to God for forgiveness.

Humility can be explained as the opposite of boastful and proud, i.e. not thinking of yourself as being better than other people.

AUTHORITY TO SAVE

Text: Luke 19:1-10

Teaching Point: Jesus has power to save men because he is God.

Memory verse: *Jesus Christ is Lord. Philippians 2 :11*

WARM-UP 1

Show the children pictures of different people cut from magazines. Include specific people as well as types. Pictures should include the monarch / head of state, a pop star, a football hero or similar, a fireman, a tramp, etc. Each time ask the children if this person is acceptable to God?

Today's true story from the Bible is about a man whom other people thought God would not want. Come back and tell me:

1. Who was the man?
2. Why did people think he was unacceptable?

CONSOLIDATION 1

The children line up down the centre of the room with the leader at the head. Tell them that you have authority over them so they must obey your commands. Designate 2 areas of the room - trees and Zacchaeus' house. Go over the responses to the various commands.

Trees	run to trees saying, swish, swish and return to centre
House	run to house and return to centre
Crowd	wag fingers saying, tut, tut
Zacchaeus	drop to knees
Jesus coming	run around on tip toe
Tax collector	rub hands together saying, lovely money

Call out the commands in random order. Children who get the command wrong miss one turn.

WIND-UP 1

Hold the wind-up in the house area from the game. Remind the children of the warm-up and go over the answers to the questions. Use the game to reinforce the meaning of having authority over someone or something. Only Jesus has power to save someone, because he is God. No one is beyond Jesus' power to save.

WARM-UP 2

Puppet sketch or skit (see page 73). Toby is making a list of the people he wants to invite to his birthday party. He goes through the list with Trudy, ending with a name she does not know. Toby explains that the final person on his list is a new boy. Trudy points out that the new boy is not from their country, but from ... (*use an appropriate country*). Trudy convinces Toby not to invite an outsider.

Today's true story from the Bible is about a man who was an outsider. No one liked him. Come back and tell me:

1. Who was the man?
2. What made him an outsider?
3. What did Jesus do for him?

CONSOLIDATION 2

Divide the children into teams of not more than 5. Prepare a set of 5 memory verse cards for each team with one word per card. The children start at one end of the room and the other end is designated as Zacchaeus' house. Place the shuffled sets of memory verse cards part way down the course. Team members take it in turns to race upright on their knees to the pile of memory verse cards, pick up a card and tip toe to Zacchaeus' house. The second child races once the first one has reached the house. Leaders can act as moving sycamore trees, obstructing older children's progress. The first team to collect their 5 cards and place them in memory verse order wins.

WIND-UP 2

Remind the children of the warm-up and go over the answers to the questions. Why did Jesus have the power to save Zacchaeus? Because he is God. Revise the memory verse.

PALM SUNDAY

Text: Luke 19:28-40

Teaching Point: Jesus came as king.

WARM-UP 1

Talk to the children about what expectations they have. What do they look forward to? Ask what they think will happen when that thing happens?

Today's true story from the Bible is about someone the people of Jesus' day were looking for. Come back and tell me:

1. What were the people looking for? [*a king*]
2. Was he obvious when he came?

CONSOLIDATION 1

Two leaders stand facing each other holding up their arms to make an arch. The children form a line and the leader designates a king by passing down the line whispering, 'you' or 'not you' to each child. The line of children passes under the arch to music. When the music stops the leaders bring down their arms to imprison the child under the arch. They ask the child if he/she is the king. If the answer is no the game continues. If the answer is yes a new king is designated in the same way as the old one was and the game continues. Periodically Leader 1 asks the children if they know who the king is. Can they recognise him/her? Is there anyone here who looks like a king?

WIND-UP 1

Remind the children about the warm-up and go over the answers to the questions. Was Jesus the obvious king? Link into the game and how difficult it was to recognise the king. How could they recognise that Jesus was God's king? The miracles he performed could not have been done by anyone other than God's king.

WARM-UP 2

Either show pictures of various modes of transport or ask leaders and/or older children to volunteer to mime them. Whether showing pictures or miming, each time ask the children to identify the mode of transport and say who drives / rides on / rides in it. Suggested transports are: ship, aeroplane, tractor, stretch limosine, train, fire engine, police car, horse, donkey, submarine, elephant, camel, spaceship. There are visual aids available on pages 88; 91; 92 and 93. For more unsual modes of transport such as limosine's and spaceships use newspaper or magazine articles or look for images on the internet or in the library.

Today's true story from the Bible is about someone who travelled in an unexpected way. Come back and tell me:

1. Who was he?
2. How did he travel?

CONSOLIDATION 2

Divide the children into 2 teams. The teams line up facing each other with an aisle in between. The children hold hands across the aisle with arms raised to make an arch (palm branches). Starting from the bottom, the first pair run up the centre beneath the arches, divide at the top and run down the outside and back to their place. They tap the next child on each side who repeats the procedure. Continue until everychild has had a turn. The first team to complete the exercise is the winner.

WIND-UP 2

Remind the children about the warm-up and go over the answers to the questions. Would the children expect a king to ride on a donkey? Jesus travelled on a donkey because he was a king coming in peace. A king arriving at a city on a horse was coming as a warrior. Link into the game and the people waving their palm branches. Why were the people so happy? Because their king had come.

THE LAST SUPPER

Text: Luke 22:1-23

Teaching Point: Jesus' death was to fulfill God's plan of salvation.

WARM-UP 1

Prepare 2 tables end to end covered with a tablecloth and with place settings for dinner for 13 people. Disposable items could be used. You also need a flip chart or similar to record the children's food and drink suggestions.

Point out the beautifully set table. Describe some of the items on the table and what they are used for. Count the number of places set. Is that a clue to the story that will follow? Ask the children what food and drink they would put on the table. Make a list.

Today we will learn about a special meal described in the Bible. How many items on the list will they get right? We will check the list after the story.

CONSOLIDATION 1

A simplified Passover meal, which takes 15-20 minutes. Each small group requires:

- 1 candle plus matches
- 3 pieces of unleavened bread (Matzot, or pitta bread if Matzot unobtainable), placed one on top of another, separated by paper napkins
- Bitter herbs - use watercress or flat leafed parsley
- Small bunch of parsley and bowl of salt water
- Charoset - use applesauce mixed with cinnamon and raisins. It represents the mortar used in slavery in Egypt.
- Roast lamb (obtainable pre-packed from some supermarkets)
- 4 cups of wine - use red juice.
- Plastic plates, napkins, paper cup.

See page 75 for detailed instructions.

WIND-UP 1

Remind the children about the warm-up and go over the list to see how many they got right. Point out how the Passover pointed forward to Jesus. This was the way God had always intended to bring people into his family.

THE LAST SUPPER

Text: Luke 22:1-23

Teaching Point: Jesus' death was to fulfill God's plan of salvation.

WARM-UP 2

Show the children pictures of various road signs and ask them to identify them (See below and page 85). Why is it important to know what the signs mean? You could also use symbols such as the poppy used to remind us what the armed forces did.

In today's true story from the Bible we will discover two special signs that Jesus left to help us remember what he did for us. Tell me later what they are.

CONSOLIDATION 2

You need a selection of prompt cards that direct the children to perform an action. Use symbols if possible. Suggestions are: jump, sit, stand, sleep, eat, ride a horse, etc. You could use some of the signs from the warm-up, such as 'one way' (for straight on), 'left turn', 'right turn', 'u-turn', etc. Demonstrate each action to be done. Have two special cards ready to lead into the wind-up. They should be a piece of bread and a cup of wine. (See page 93) When these are displayed the children say, 'Thank you Lord Jesus'.

WIND-UP 2

Remind the children about the warm-up and go over the answer to the question. Display the bread and cup signs. Talk about the importance of signs that help us to remember things. Explain that we still use those signs in the Lord's Supper to help us remember what Jesus has done for us and how this was always God's plan.

THE CRUCIFIXION

Text: Luke 23:13-43

Teaching Point: Jesus died in my place.

WARM-UP 1

Ask the children to write down on paper some of their sins from this last week - specific detail and not generalised platitudes. The younger children will need help with this. Collect the pieces of paper, place in a bucket and build a hill over it. Seal everything up tightly.

Ask the children if they think this is a good way to deal with their sins (the naughty things they do)? Will it take them away? Today's true story from the Bible is about the way God took away our sins. Come back and tell me how he did it.

CONSOLIDATION 1

Divide the children into teams. For each team prepare a set of colour coded cards containing the following statements:

1. Jesus died because he was guilty.
2. Jesus died because Pilate had more power.
3. Jesus died because his friends could not rescue him.
4. Jesus died for nothing.
5. Jesus died because he was in the wrong place at the wrong time.
6. Jesus died because Judas was a better planner.
7. Jesus died so that I could be friends with God.
8. Jesus died to pay the price for the bad things I do.
9. Jesus died because he was weak.
10. Jesus died because he did not speak up for himself.
11. Jesus died because he walked into a trap.
12. Jesus died so that I might live.
13. Jesus died because it was part of God's perfect plan.
14. Jesus died so that God's love for me could be shown.
15. Jesus died because he wanted people to feel sorry for him.

Either hide the cards around the room for the children to find the 15 cards of their colour, or run a race with team members taking it in turns to run the length of the room, pick up a card and return to base. Once all 15 cards have been collected the children must sort them into true and false statements.

WIND-UP 1

Remind the children about the warm-up and open up the hill to see if their sins have been taken away. Was this a good way to deal with sin? What was God's way. Use the cards collected in the game to make sure that they understand why Jesus had to die.

Lesson 26

THE CRUCIFIXION

Text: Luke 23:13-43

Teaching Point: Jesus died in my place.

WARM-UP 2

Leader 1 dresses up as a football team captain and tells the children about an imaginary football game. Both sides were evenly matched. First the opposing team scored, then we scored. Our star player was injured and had to be stretchered off. Everyone on our side was devastated. How could we manage without him? We were bound to lose. The substitute came on and do you know what happened? The ball was passed back to him and he dribbled it up the field and scored the winning goal. Everyone cheered. He was even better than our star player. Just as well he was substituted. The other team were really fed up.

Today's true story from the Bible is about someone else who was a substitute and saved the day. Come back and tell me:

1. Who was he?
2. For whom did he substitute?

CONSOLIDATION 2

Play a rescue game. Divide the children into teams and give each team a plastic sledge or washing basket attached to a rope. The teams start at one end of the room and a leader stands at the other. The older children take it in turns to pull the sledges. Team members are pulled one at a time to safety at the other end of the room where the child in the sledge has to give the password to be allowed in. The password is, 'In my place.' The first team to get all its members to safety wins. Continue until all the children are safe.

WIND-UP 2

Remind the children about the warm-up and go over the answers to the questions. Link into the game and the use of the password, 'In my place.' Make sure that the children understand that Jesus died for them, to take their punishment, so that they can be made right with God and be part of his family.

THE RESURRECTION

Text: Luke 24:1-35

Teaching Point: Jesus rose from the dead so that we can know he is God.

Memory verse: *Christ died for our sins, as is written in the Scriptures. 1 Corinthians 15:3*

WARM-UP 1

How do I know whether to believe someone? Show the children a treasure chest or large box with some things connected to the story, some not. Say that all the contents are connected to the story. Bring out items one by one. How will they know whether I have told the truth? Listen carefully to the story to see if I have.

CONSOLIDATION 1

Divide the children into teams. Prepare a set of memory verse words per team. Collect enough lidded containers for each word plus 3 or 4 per team. Place a word or a blank piece of paper in each container. Place the containers in the centre of the room under a sheet supported by tables. Children run to the containers one at a time, pick up a container and return to base. As soon as a child returns the next child runs. If the container has a word, keep the word and container. If there is no word (or one already collected) return the container to the centre with the next child to run. Keep going until all the words and reference are collected. The winning team is the first to collect all the words and put them in order.

WIND-UP 1

Go over the items in the treasure chest. Which were part of the story? Did I tell the truth? How do you know? What did Jesus tell his disciples before he died? Was that true? How do we know? What is the result? Our sins taken away and heaven when we die. Revise memory verse.

WARM-UP 2

Place a large box on a table and bring out the items one by one. Each time ask the children if they know what the item is and what it proves about the holder. Suggested items are sports trophies, certificates for ballet, music, etc. showing a certain skill level has been acheived, a birthday card to a named person showing what age has been reached, a passport. If the sports trophies and certificates do not celebrate the leader's achievements, ask the children, 'Do you think I did this?' Ask an older child to read out the name on the trophy or certificate. Point out that all the items prove something about the person who is named.

Today's true story from the Bible is about an event that proved something about someone. Come back and tell me:

1. What was the event?
2. What did it prove?

CONSOLIDATION 2

Prepare some true and false statements. The children line up down the centre of the room facing the leader. The leader reads out statements one by one. After each has been read the children must decide if it is true or false. If true they run to the right wall and back to the centre, if false they run to the left wall and back to the centre. (Right for right and left for lie.) Any who run the wrong way go to the sin bin. Periodically the leader calls out, 'The Cross,' at which point all in the sin bin can rejoin the game.

WIND-UP 2

Remind the children about the warm-up and go over the answers to the questions. Refer to the game. What was the only way the people in the sin bin could be released? Through the cross. Jesus rising from the dead proves he is God and that his death on the cross paid the penalty for our sins (the naughty things we do).

POWER PROMISED

Text: Luke 24:45-53, Acts 1:1-11

Teaching Point: Jesus promised to send his Holy Spirit.

WARM-UP 1

Skit or puppets (see page 77).

Trudy is running for class captain/prefect. She has to make a speech to her classmates to encourage them to vote for her. She asks Toby to listen to it. Trudy makes a speech containing all sorts of promises, which get more and more impossible to fulfil. Toby points this out, but Trudy will not listen to him.

Today's true story from the Bible is about a promise. Come back and tell me:

1. What was the promise?
2. Who made the promise?
3. Where would the promise take place?

CONSOLIDATION 1

Prepare 8 cards and write one of the following letters on each: P R O M I S E D. Write the following 3 words on the back of each letter: What? Who? Where? Divide the children into teams of not more than 8. Stick the 8 cards around the walls. The leader calls out the 8 letters in random order and the method to be used to retrieve it (see below). Each time a letter is called out, a member of each team races in the designated style to that letter. The first one there takes the letter for his/her team. A different team member must race each time. Once all team members have raced start at the beginning again.

Suggested retrieval methods: run, jump keeping legs together, crawl, holding onto ankles, walk, bunny hop, on all fours (hands and feet), tip toes. For a smallish group all the team members could run at the same time to retrieve the final letter.

The winning team is the one that collects the most letters.

WIND-UP 1

Remind the children about the warm-up and go over the answers to the questions. Did Toby believe Trudy would keep her promises? Why not? The disciples knew Jesus would keep his promise, because he had always kept his promises in the past. Ask the children to hold up the letters collected in the game. Ask them to place them in the order to spell a word. Once they have spelt 'promised' ask 3 of them to read out the words on the back. Use these to revise the answers to the warm-up questions.

POWER PROMISED

Text: Luke 24:45-53, Acts 1:1-11

Teaching Point: 'Jesus is in heaven and one day will return.'

WARM-UP 2

Tell the children that you promise to give them a piece of cake or homemade biscuit. First of all you must make it. Put on an apron and display the recipe. Get out the ingredients, scales, mixing bowl, etc. and place on a table in clear view of the children. Ask the children to read out the list of ingredients and check that you have everything. Ask them to read out the method and follow their instructions. Once the cake or biscuit mix is ready place in the appropriate container for baking. Point out that you cannot keep your promise straight away because the cake or biscuits need to be baked before they can be eaten.

Today's true story from the Bible is about a promise. Come back and tell me:

1. What was the promise? [*Jesus will return*]
2. Who made it?
3. Did it come true? [*Not yet*]

While the children are at Bibletime bake the cake or biscuits if you have the appropriate facilities. If not, bring some that you have baked at home.

CONSOLIDATION 2

The object of the game is to teach that they might have to wait for a promise to be fulfilled. Tell the children to hide and promise to come and find them. Count slowly to 50 while they hide. Do not attempt to find them. Eventually they will start to peep out to see where you are. At that point call out, 'Change!' and count slowly to 50 while they find a new hiding place. Repeat several times. After the last call go and find the children.

WIND-UP 2

Talk about the game. The children hid but no one came until the last time of hiding. Did they get fed up with waiting? Remind them about the warm-up and go over the answers to the questions. Have you kept your promise? They had to wait. Hand out a piece of cake or biscuit to each child. Jesus promised that he will come back again. We can trust him to keep that promise and must wait patiently. Meanwhile he has given us his Holy Spirit to be with us until he comes again.

Lesson 28

POWER GIVEN

Text: Acts 1:4-9; 2:1-41

Teaching Point: Jesus sends his Spirit to enable us to be his witnesses.

Memory verse: *God's Spirit lives in you! 1 Corinthians 3:16*

WARM-UP 1

Ask four volunteers to perform simple activities such as running on the spot, star jumps, cycling in the air or clapping. Each volunteer demontrates one action for the group to perform.

Ask the volunteers, 'Are you alive? How do we know?' (refer back to their actions). Ask the children, 'Do you know what keeps you alive?' Deal with their answers, ending with blood being the thing that keeps you alive. Prick your or another leader's finger to demonstrate the blood. You cannot normally see my blood, so how do you know I'm alive? By my actions (refer back to the activities).

What did Jesus promise to give to his disciples in last week's lesson? The Holy Spirit.

Could the disciples see the Holy Spirit?

What did Jesus say that the Holy Spirit would help his disciples do? Tell people about Jesus.

In today's true story from the Bible we will see what happened when Jesus kept that promise. Come back and tell me:

1. Where were the disciples when the promise came true?
2. How did they know the promise had come true?
3. What was the result? [*Peter told people about Jesus and 3,000 were converted.*]

Lesson 29

CONSOLIDATION 1

Divide into equal number teams. Make 4 staging posts or compounds in a large circle. Prepare 1 strip of paper for each team containing the words of the memory verse. Roll the memory verse strips into a scroll. Number off each team 1 to 4. All No.1's go to the first staging post, No.2's to the second staging post, etc. On the command to start one child of each team leaves the first staging post and runs to the second, taking their memory verse scroll with them. When the child reaches the second staging post he/she hands the scroll to a child of the same team, who runs to third, and so on round the circle until all team members have changed to the next staging post. The winning team is the first one to get all their members to their next post.

NB One leader should be posted at each staging post to see fair play. Work out beforehand which is the winning post.

WIND-UP 1

Refer back to the warm-up. How do we know someone's alive? Go over the answers to the warm-up questions. How do we know the Holy Spirit lives in us?

What did Holy Spirit come to do? Remind the children of the game - taking the message from place to place.

POWER GIVEN

Text: Acts 1:4-9; 2:1-41

Teaching Point: Jesus sends his Spirit to enable us to be his witnesses.

Memory verse: *God's Spirit lives in you! 1 Corinthians 3:16*

WARM-UP 2

The aim of the warm-up is to demonstrate different forms of power. Suggestions are:

- wind power - blow a piece of paper or a balloon from point to point.
- electric power - turn on a lamp or similar plugged into the mains.
- strength - lift a heavy weight.
- authority (power over) - tell the children to stand up, then sit down, repeating several times.

Today's true story from the Bible is about a different type of power. Come back and tell me:

1. Who was given power?
2. When did they get it?
3. What did the power enable them to do?

Alternatively, build a wall from boxes down the centre of the room and give the children rolled up newspaper sheets. Ask them to knock down the wall with newspaper. They do not have the power to do it. Today's true story from the Bible is about people who were given power to do something. Use the same questions as above.

CONSOLIDATION 2

Divide the group into teams of not more than 10 children. Divide each team in half, placing them at opposite ends of the room. Each half team must have a leader or older child. The aim is to take the following message from place to place: 'The Holy Spirit helps us to tell others about Jesus.' The team leader at one end has the words, *The, Spirit, us, tell, about,'* and the team leader at the other end has the remaining 5 words. Designate which end of the room is the start. On the command to start the team leader at the start end tells child A the first word. Child A runs to the other end and repeats that word to the team. The team leader at that end tells child B the next word and child B runs to the other end and repeats that word to the team. While child B is running the team writes down the word brought by child A. Continue until all team members and words have changed ends. If there are less team members than words some team members will run twice. Once all words have changed ends the two half teams join forces to put the words in order of the message.

WIND-UP 2

Remind the children about the warm-up. Could they see the power source? How did they know the power was present? They saw the results. Go over the answers to the warm-up questions. Refer to the game. What was the message? Why did Jesus send his Holy Spirit? To give us the power to tell others about Jesus.

esson 29

PETER HEALING THE LAME MAN

Text: Acts 3:1-26

Teaching Point: The need to have faith in Jesus.

WARM-UP 1

Display a collection of boxes, cartons, packets and tins, some with well-known brand names such as Kellogg's Corn Flakes, Pringles Crisps, Cadbury's chocolates, Cadbury's Chocolate Finger Biscuits, Weetabix, etc., and some wrapped up in brown paper and marked on the outside 'No Frills' Crummy corn flakes (powdered), Smelly sprout and curry flavoured crisps, Severed finger biscuits, Putrid stale block chocolates, Stale wheat straw blocks, etc. Ask the children to choose which ones they would prefer. Why is the name important?

Ask the children how many of them have brand name clothing? Why is the name important?

In today's true story from the Bible we will learn about a man being changed through a name. Come back and tell me:

1. What was the name?
2. What happened through that name?

CONSOLIDATION 1

Provide each child with a mat or piece of newspaper to represent a mat. (Carpet shops often have sample books that they are willing to donate.) On the underside of about 1/3 of them write or stick the name, 'Jesus'. Scatter the mats around the room. The children move around to music. When the music stops everyone must stand on a mat. The leader indicates 1-5 children, depending on the number in the group. Everyone indicated must look under their mat. If 'Jesus' is on the underside they are safe and remain in the game. All those indicated with nothing under their mats are out and must take their mats to the side of the room and sit on them, like the lame man. After every 3-4 turns the leader calls out, 'In the name of Jesus, walk!' and all those who are out rejoin the game, placing their mats on the floor in the playing area.

WIND-UP 1

Remind the children about the warm-up and go over the answers to the warm-up questions. Refer to the game to reinforce the importance of the name of Jesus and what happened through his name.

PETER HEALING THE LAME MAN

Text: Acts 3:1-26

Teaching Point: The need to have faith in Jesus.

Memory verse: *For even the Son of Man did not come to be served, but to serve, and to give his life as a ransom for many. Mark 10:45*

WARM-UP 2

Prior to the lesson write a selection of tasks, one per card, for the children to perform with or without assistance. Suggested tasks are:

1. Lift a chair up by one leg starting with four legs on the ground.
2. Unwind a ball of string so that when you hold it by one end and it is straight it will not touch the floor.
3. Pick up and hold 7 tennis balls using your hands only.
4. Balance 3 bottles on your head.
5. Take two disposable cups and stand on them without collapsing them.
6. With envelopes on both hands open a sealed envelope.

Ask for 3 volunteers from the children to choose a task by picking one of the cards. If they cannot perform the task they are allowed to ask anyone for help.

Once the tasks have been completed discuss why they asked particular people for help. In today's true story from the Bible a man needed help. Come back and tell me:

1. Why did he need help?
2. Whom did he ask for help?
3. Did he get the help he was expecting?

CONSOLIDATION 2

Divide the group into teams and prepare a set of 11 memory verse cards for each team. On each card write a different part of the memory verse, including the reference (see the lines between the words of the verse below). The teams start at one end of the room and the memory verse cards are shuffled and placed at the other end with an obstacle course in between (see diagram).

The team members take it in turns to shuffle on their bottoms as far as the gateway, walk to the next marker and leap along from there to the end. When they reach the end they pick up a memory verse card and run back to the start. The second team member does not run until the first one has returned. The winning team is the first one to collect their memory verse cards and place them in Bible verse order.

Memory verse: *For even / the Son / of Man / did not come / to be served, / but to serve, / and to give / his life / as a ransom / for many. / Mark 10:45*

WIND-UP 2

Remind the children about the warm-up and who needed help. Go over the answers to the warm-up questions. What help did the lame man receive? How was he healed? Refer to the game to reinforce story detail. Revise the memory verse.

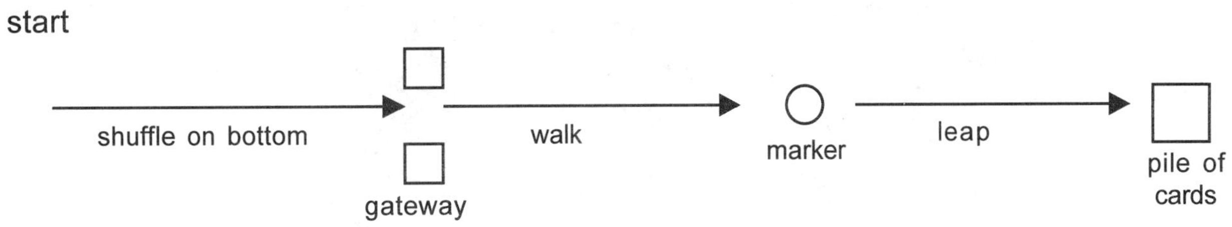

PREACHING THE GOSPEL

Text: Acts 8:1-6,26-40

Teaching Point: The importance of telling others about Jesus.

WARM-UP 1

Prior to the session write the following message on a piece of paper using symbols for words: 'How can I understand what I am reading unless someone explains it to me?' Use symbols that can be read out to the children, such as red square, green circle, blue triangle. You need 13 symbols. Prepare 14 cards with one word of the message on each card and draw the appropriate symbol on the back of each card ('I' will have the same symbol on both cards). Tape the sheet of paper containing the message inside a book and hide the 14 cards around the room.

Say you have come across a book, which looks exciting, but you can't understand it. Open the book and read out the message. Can the children understand it? You need help. You need to find out what the symbols mean. Ask them to search for the 14 cards with symbols on. Once they are found read out the message and ask an older child to pin the symbols in order onto a board. Turn them over to discover the meaning.

In today's true story from the Bible someone needed help to understand what he was reading:

1. Who was the man?
2. What was he reading?
3. Who helped him understand it?

CONSOLIDATION 1

Place a large sheet or parachute on the floor in the middle of the room to be the chariot. It must be big enough to contain all the children and leaders. Designate an area at one side of the room as the river. The leader calls out the following commands in random order, using each command several times.

- chariot - get into the chariot
- scatter - run to the sides of the room
- water - run to the river area.

After each command the leader asks, 'Why did … (they scatter / Philip get into the chariot / they get into the water)?' Use 'water' as the last command and cover everyone at the river with the sheet to symbolise going under the water.

WIND-UP 1

Have the wind-up under the sheet or parachute. Remind the children about the warm-up and go over the answers to the questions. The older children should know which part of the Bible the Ethiopian was reading (Isaiah). Refer to the game and go over the questions asked following each command.

PREACHING THE GOSPEL

Text: Acts 8:1-6,26-40

Teaching Point: The importance of telling others about Jesus.

Memory verse: *God's Spirit lives in you. 1 Corinthians 3:16*

WARM-UP 2

Leader 2 tells the children that he is in charge today and Leader 1 has told him that he has to be like him (Leader 1). Leader 2 opens a box and brings out some clothes so that he can dress up to be like Leader 1. He makes a mess of it and asks the children to help him to get it right.

Leader 2 tells the children that Leader 1 has asked him to do a special job, measuring the room. Leader 2 gets out a tape measure and tries to measure the front of the room from side to side. He is unsuccessful because he cannot hold both ends of the tape in place at the same time. He needs a helper. Leader 2 measures the front of the room using the children to help.

In today's true story from the Bible we will find out about someone who needed a helper. Come back and tell me:

1. Who needed a helper?
2. Who was the helper?
3. How did he help?
4. Who was the special helper who helped the man who gave the help?

CONSOLIDATION 2

The aim is to take God's word (the memory verse) from Location A to Location B. Divide the group into teams of not more than 9 children. For each team prepare a set of 9 cards, each one containing one word of the memory verse including the reference.

The children take it in turns to run to A and pick up one word of the memory verse. Then they are piggy backed by a leader to Location B. The winner is the first team to get all their memory verse cards to B and put them in the correct order.

WIND-UP 2

Remind the children about the warm-up; Leader 2 needed a helper to be like Leader 1 and to do the job Leader 1 had given to him. Refer to the game. The children could only get from A to B by piggy back, so they needed a helper. Go over the answers to the warm-up questions. The Ethiopian needed a helper and Philip needed a helper (the Holy Spirit). The Holy Spirit helped Philip to tell the Ethiopian about Jesus. The Holy Spirit helps us to be like Jesus and to tell others about him (Jesus).

PAUL'S CONVERSION

Text: Acts 9:1-25

Teaching point: Conversion results in a changed life.

WARM-UP 1

The aim is to demonstrate that many things around us have changed dramatically from their original state. Suggestions are:

- a carton of pure fruit juice and an orange.
- a piece of wooden furniture and a picture of a tree.
- a woollen garment and a sheep (soft toy or picture of a sheep - see page 91)
- a cotton garment and some cotton wool rolled into a ball to look like raw cotton on the bush.
- a metal object and a stone that could represent iron ore.
- a newspaper and a picture of a tree (or just a blank piece of paper).

Display the finished articles on one table and the objects demonstrating their original state on another table. Pick up the finished articles in turn and ask the children, 'How do you think this item started life?' or, 'Where do you think this came from?' Once the children have identified the correct original object place it beside the finished article. When all articles have been paired up ask the children, 'Did these items change themselves or were they changed by some other force?'

Today's true story from the Bible is about a person who was changed. Come back and tell me:

1. Who was changed?
2. How was he changed?
3. Who did the changing?

CONSOLIDATION 1

Place 4 area markers around the room so that they are roughly the same distance from each other. These can be dens marked out by chairs or sheets/parachutes for the children to get under. Set aside an area for the children found at the wrong location. The children stand in the centre of the room so that they can see the 4 designated areas and the exclusion zone. Point out the 4 areas and the exclusion zone. Instruct the children to choose one of the 4 areas and go there to wait for further instructions. When they are in position tell them the rules of the game. When the leader shouts 'Change!' everyone is to leave their area and run as fast as possible to another area. The leader will then nominate one of the areas to be out and all the children in that area will go off to the exclusion zone and miss a turn. To add some variety to the game the leader can shout 'Change!' a few times in quick succession so that the children have to run around without stopping. If the children are old enough they could be instructed to hop, skip, bunny-hop, roll, walk backwards, hold ankles while walking, run on all fours, etc. to the next area.

WIND-UP 1

Remind the children about the warm-up and how much the items had changed. Refer to the game and how they had to change from one place to another. Go over the answers to the warm-up questions. Did Paul change in the same way as the warm-up items or by moving to a different place? God changed Paul on the inside and made him a new person. Instead of persecuting Christians Paul told other people they should become Christians and follow Jesus.

PAUL'S CONVERSION

Text: Acts 9:1-25

Teaching point: Conversion results in a changed life.

WARM-UP 2

Place 4 sets of dressing up clothes on a table at the front of the room. Ask for 4 volunteers to get dressed up. Once the volunteers have put on the dressing up clothes ask for a further 4 volunteers. Pair up the new volunteers with the old ones. On the command, 'Change!' the children have to take off their dressing up clothes and change with their partner before the remaining children can count to 50 slowly.

Today's true story from the Bible is about a person who changed. Come back and tell me:

1. Who changed?
2. How did he change?
3. Who did the changing?

CONSOLIDATION 2

The object is to take every day articles and change their appearance so that it is difficult to recognise what they were originally. Divide the children into groups and give each group a separate area of the room to work in. Each group should have the same number of articles to disguise, but a different selection. Provide each group with newspaper, pieces of cloth, sticky tape and string. After a set time limit the groups display their disguised articles. If another group can guess what the article is that group gets a point. If no one can guess the article the group that disguised it gets a point.

WIND-UP 2

Remind the children about the warm-up and go over the answers to the questions. Refer to the game. Did Paul change in the same way as the items in the game? God changed Paul on the inside and made him a new person. Instead of persecuting Christians Paul told other people they should become Christians and follow Jesus.

Lesson 32

PETER RAISING DORCAS TO LIFE

Text: Acts 9:31-43

Teaching Point: The true response to miracles is belief in Jesus.

WARM-UP 1

Show the children an object and destroy it. Suggestions are:

- wrap an old plate in a towel and break it into pieces with a hammer *(take extra care with this one)*
- tear a newspaper into small pieces
- cut a picture or poster into pieces
- damage an already broken toy.

After destroying the object, ask, 'What shall I do with this now? Is it any good?' Ask if you should repair it? If they say yes, tell them that you cannot repair it because you do not have anything with which to make the repair. Then ask, 'If we just leave it here, will it become new again?' End by saying that the situation is hopeless and throw the object into a bin.

Today's true story from the Bible is about someone who did not see the situation as hopeless. Come back and tell me:

1. Who was he?
2. What was the situation?
3. What did he do about it?

CONSOLIDATION 1

A leader(s) is designated as 'It' and given a soft sponge ball. 'It' tries to tag the children below the shoulders with the sponge ball while they move around the room. Any child tagged falls to the ground dead. A leader designated as Peter moves around the room giving each 'dead' child a piece of ribbon or similar, at which point the 'dead' child gets up and rejoins the game.

NB If there are a large number of children it might be better for tagged children to move to the side of the room before falling down dead, so that other children do not trip over them.

WIND-UP 1

Remind the children about the warm-up and go over the answers to the questions. Refer to the game. Count the ribbons to see how many children were made alive. What happened as a result of Dorcas coming back to life? Many people in the area believed in Jesus.

WARM-UP 2

Place a box at the front containing sufficient adult clothing to dress up 3-4 children. Ask for volunteers to be dressed up. Leaders dress up the children, asking the other children to help choose the items. Judge the results.

Today's true story from the Bible is about someone who made clothes for people. Come back and tell me:

1. What was her name?
2. What happened to her?

CONSOLIDATION 2

Divide the children into teams. For each team prepare a box of clothing with 1 item per team member. Suggested clothing: hat, scarf, gloves, shirt(s), jumper(s), coat. Place the boxes at the opposite end of the room from the children. On the command to start the first team member runs to the other end of the room, picks an item of clothing, puts it on and runs back to their team. They take it off and hand the clothing to the second team member, who puts it on, runs to the box, picks another item of clothing, puts it on and races back to their team. Both items of clothing are donned by the third team member, who repeats the exercise. Continue until all team members have run. The final team member will end up dressed in all the clothes.

NB Clever teams will send their youngest members first.

WIND-UP 2

Refer to the game and dressing up. Who made clothes in the Bible story? Remind the children about the warm-up and go over the answers to the questions. What happened as a result of Dorcas coming back to life? Many people in the area believed in Jesus.

TAKING THE GOSPEL TO THE GENTILES

Text: Acts 10:1-48

Teaching Point: The gospel is for everyone, regardless of race, colour or creed.

WARM-UP 1

Choose several people to receive awards. Suggested categories are: long service, helpfulness, cheerfulness, best behaved, well dressed, etc. As each category and winner is read out, that person comes out and receives a certificate. (Give each chosen leader a bag of sweets as well. These should be shared with their group at Bibletime, although the children do not know this at this point.) Once they have been applauded they return to their seats. The people chosen to receive the awards do not necessarily fulfil the criteria, e.g. the person receiving the long service award could be a relatively new member of the group. After the chosen people have resumed their seats ask the children if what you did was fair? Why not?

In today's true story from the Bible we will learn about something that was for everyone, not just a few. Come back and tell me what it was.

CONSOLIDATION 1

Prepare 6 cards with different statements about the group, one per card. Suggested statements are: anyone with brown shoes, anyone with blond hair, anyone with white socks, anyone with blue eyes, anyone with black shoes, anyone who is over 5ft. 6ins tall. Make sure that everyone is included in at least one statement.

The children and leaders form a circle holding hands. The circle moves round in a clockwise direction until the command is given to freeze. This could be done to music, stopping the music to stop the circle, or by calling out, 'Gentiles!' One of the children chooses an envelope and reads out the statement. All those that qualify form a smaller circle within the large circle. Repeat, with the 2 circles moving in opposite directions, until all 6 statements have been read out. By the end everyone should have transferred from the outside circle to the inside one. When the inside circle becomes bigger than the outside one the people in the outside circle stop holding hands.

WIND-UP 1

Remind the children about the warm-up and go over the answer to the question. The good news about Jesus is not just for a few people, but for everyone. How does God choose people? Does he choose people in the way they were chosen in the game? God's salvation is not just for some people who live in certain countries or who have a certain colour skin. God wants all people to be made right with him and join his family.

TAKING THE GOSPEL TO THE GENTILES

Text: Acts 10:1-48

Teaching Point: The gospel is for everyone, regardless of race, colour or creed.

WARM-UP 2

Take an old telephone directory containing residential numbers. Tell the children what it is. Tear out one page for each child, taking the pages from different areas of the directory. Ask some of the older children to read out some of the names from their pages. Tell the children they must keep the pages safe because they will need them for the game.

Today's true story from the Bible is about something that was for everyone, not just a few. Come back and tell me what it was.

CONSOLIDATION 2

Tear up the remainder of the telephone directory and hide the pages around the area. The children search for the pages and spread them out on the floor so that they can put them back into the right order. They will need to contribute the pages they were given in the warm-up.

For larger groups, divide into teams and give each team a block of page numbers to collect. Once the blocks have been collated, ask children from other teams to give their pages to the appropriate teams. Go round each group asking, 'Is the good news about Jesus for these people?'

WIND-UP 2

Remind the children about the warm-up and go over the answer to the question. Point out that the telephone directory just contains the names of people on the telephone in a certain area. What happened in the game when the directory was incomplete? They had to hand over their pages of names. The good news about Jesus is for everyone, everywhere. Our contribution is to tell our friends about Jesus and ask them to come with us to hear about him.

PETER IN PRISON

Text: Acts 12:1-19

Teaching Point: God looks after his people in all circumstances.

WARM-UP 1

Before the session place a selection of similarly shaped objects on a table and cover with a sheet e.g. a football, an inverted bowl with a rounded base, a hat with a round top and an inflated balloon. Count the number of objects present under the sheet and ask the children to identify them. If they need help, turn the sheet back to show a little bit of the object. Once the object has been correctly identified turn the sheet back to display it. Point out that they did not know what the objects were, but you did because you put them there. Did the children expect those objects to be on the table? Sometimes things are not where we expect them to be, but that does not mean that they are in the wrong place. Today's true story from the Bible is about someone who was in a place where he did not want to be. Come back and tell me:

1. What was his name?
2. Where was he?
3. How did he get out?

CONSOLIDATION 1

Make 4 prisons around the room, marking the boundaries with chairs or similar. The children scatter into the 4 prisons. On the command, 'Angel!' they run to a different prison. After 2-3 turns designate one of the prisons as the secure one. Anyone in that prison must remain there. Thereafter, randomly pick one of the remaining 3 prisons after each turn and all children in that prison must move to the secure one. Continue until all the children have transferred to the secure prison. If time allows, rerun the game, choosing a different prison to be the secure one.

WIND-UP 1

Remind the children about the warm-up and go over the answers to the questions. The leader knew what was under the sheet because he had put the objects there. God knew that Peter was in prison and God rescued him. Refer to the game. How did Peter get out of prison? God sent an angel to rescue him. God is in control and he knows what is happening to us. God always looks after us.

WARM-UP 2

A skit or puppets (see script on page 78). Toby and Trudy are getting ready to go to camp or on a residential school trip. It is the first time they have gone away without their parents. Trudy is very anxious about this. What will happen if she does not like the food or is ill or cannot sleep, etc. Toby reassures her that he will be there and he will help her.

Today's true story from the Bible is about someone who ended up in a difficult situation. Come back and tell me:

1. What was his name?
2. Where was he?
3. How did he get out?

CONSOLIDATION 2

Divide the children into groups of boys and girls and place each group at opposite ends of the room. Mark out an area at the side of the room to be the prison. Designate 1-2 leaders as 'It'. Boys are called 'Peter' and girls are 'Rhoda'. When the leader calls, 'Peter' the boys race to the other end of the room. If a leader manages to tag a child that child goes to prison. The same thing happens when 'Rhoda' is called. The leader calls out the names randomly. Periodically the leader calls out, 'Angel!', at which point all those children in prison are released to rejoin the game.

WIND-UP 2

Remind the children about the warm-up and go over the answers to the questions. Trudy had Toby to be with her and help her. Whom did Peter have? How did God rescue Peter? Refer to the game and how they were released from prison. Why were the girls called Rhoda? What part did she play in the story?

PAUL AT PHILIPPI

Text: Acts 16:1-22

Teaching Point: God wants people everywhere to learn about Jesus.

Memory verse: *God commands all people to repent. Acts 17:30*

WARM-UP 1

If possible use a ball with a map of the world on it. Form a circle and throw the ball from person to person. When the leader blows a whistle the person holding the ball points to a country on it. The child (or leader if the child cannot read) identifies the country. Ask, 'Do you think the people who live there need to learn about Jesus? Say a short prayer for the people of that country. Continue for several countries. If you do not have a globe ball use a normal ball and a map of the world. When the whistle blows the child holding the ball goes to the map and points to a country.

Ask the children if they can remember whom they learned about the previous week? Paul lived in Antioch. Show roughly where this is on the map. In today's true story from the Bible we will see how the good news about Jesus got to some people living in this place (point to the region of Philippi). Come back and tell me:

1. How did God tell Paul where to go?
2. Who was the first person to listen to Paul at Philippi?
3. What happened to Paul at the end of the story?

CONSOLIDATION 1

Divide the children into teams. For each child prepare a strip of paper containing the memory verse. The children start at one end of the room (Antioch) and race to the other end (Philippi), traversing some obstacles on the way (see diagram).

At Lystra place a box of miscellaneous small items to represent Timothy. The aim is for each child to take the message (their memory verse strip) from Antioch to Philippi, picking up Timothy on the way.

The team members take it tin turns to run to Lystra, pick up 'Timothy', run to Troas, zig-zagging to avoid 2 obstacles (chairs), get into a boat (plastic sledge or laundrey basket) and be pulled to Philippi. The second child runs as soon as the first child reaches Philippi. The winning team is the first one to get all its members from Antioch to Philippi.

WIND-UP 1

Remind the children about the warm-up. God wants everyone to hear the good news about Jesus. They can only hear if someone tells them. Go over the answers to the warm-up questions. Refer to the game for how Paul got the message from Antioch to Philippi. The people in Philippi heard the message because Paul listened to God and did what God said.

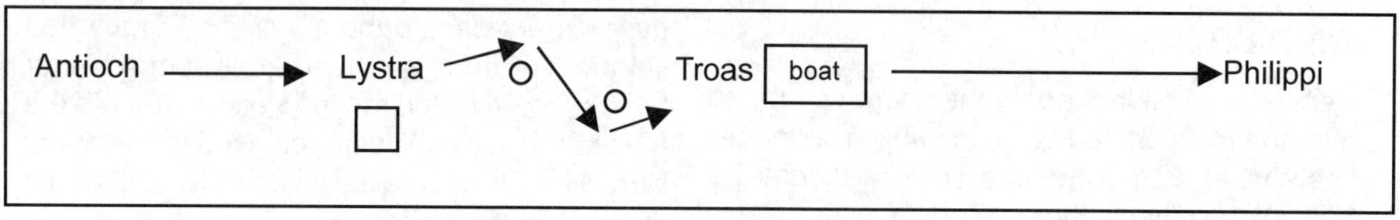

PAUL AT PHILIPPI

Text: Acts 16:1-22

Teaching Point: God wants people everywhere to learn about Jesus.

Memory verse: *God commands all people to repent. Acts 17:30*

WARM-UP 2

Prepare a large box full of a variety of small items that make a noise when shaken. Include a strip of paper containing the following message, 'Come and help us!' Wrap up the box in paper and place it under a table at the front. Tell the children that you are expecting a special parcel. Have they seen it? When they say it is under the table, look under another table or elsewhere. Eventually you will see it. Try to open it under the table without success. Prime Leader 2 to tell you to take it out from under the table and place it on top. Instead of sliding the box out and placing it on the table, roll the table over so that the table top is laid on its front edge with the legs pointing away from the children. Pick up the box and try to place it on the edge of the table. Ask someone for help. Leader 2 helps put the table back to the upright position. Place the box on the table and ask the children what to do next. When they tell you to open the paper place the box on one side, cut out the base, and turn it back upright without spilling the contents. Is this the right way to open a parcel? Lift the box up slowly by the top so that the contents spill out onto the table. Pick out the message and read it out.

Today's true story from the Bible is about some people who needed help. Come back and tell me:

1. How did Paul know the people needed help?
2. What help did they need?

CONSOLIDATION 2

Divide the children into teams of not more than 7 children plus a team leader (an older child or leader). Each team needs a large piece of paper with a man's head in the middle and 7 speech bubbles cut from card with one word from the following sentence on each: 'Come over to Macedonia and help us.' Give each team leader a set of 7 questions and answers from the Bible passage. (See page 84)

The team leader asks a question and, when the correct answer is given, one of the team members runs to the other end of the room, picks up a speech bubble and returns to base. Continue until all 7 bubbles have been collected. The winning team is the first one to collect all their speech bubbles and glue them in the correct order around the man's head.

WIND-UP 2

Refer to the game and to the request from the man at Macedonia. Remind the children about the warm-up. Was this the kind of help the man needed? The people needed to hear the good news about Jesus so that they could be made right with God and become part of his family.

PAUL IN PRISON

Text: Acts 16:23-40

Teaching Point: God was with Paul, even in prison.

WARM-UP 1

With the help of some older children tie up a leader (or volunteer adult) with rope so that he is completely immobilised. Legs should be tied together and arms roped to his sides. Place the captive in a 'cell' and cover the cell with a sheet. Point out that he cannot escape.

In today's true story from the Bible someone is chained up in prison to stop them escaping. Come back and tell me:

1. Who was he?
2. Why was he in prison?
3. How did he escape from his chains?

Once the children have gone to Bibletime untie the captive, who stays out of sight until the beginning of the consolidation. Leave the ropes in the cell and recover with the sheet.

CONSOLIDATION 1

Before the game starts ask the children what they expect to find in the prison cell? Uncover the cell to see what is there. The captive has escaped, leaving the ropes behind. The captive reappears at this point.

Designate an area to be the prison. Play a game where children are captured, such as tag or run the gauntlet, where the children run the length of the room with the leaders attempting to hit them below the shoulders with a soft ball. Any child who is tagged goes to prison. Periodically the leader calls out, 'Earthquake!' and everyone stops and jumps up and down. Everyone in prison is released and the game restarts.

WIND-UP 1

Remind the children about the warm-up and go over the answers to the questions. Who was with Paul (apart from Silas!)? God was with Paul, even in prison. How did God release Paul? Through an earthquake. Refer to the game. What happened as a result of Paul going to prison? The gaoler believed in Jesus and was saved.

Lesson 37

PAUL IN PRISON

Text: Acts 16:23-40

Teaching Point: God was with Paul, even in prison.

WARM-UP 2

Tell the children that a friend is in prison and you want to get him out. How can you do it? You are due to visit him and want to take in the necessary equipment. Ask them for suggestions and record them on a board. Where possible show articles or pictures of each suggestion. Suggested ways are:

- a hacksaw in a loaf of bread
- a key
- a rope to climb over the wall
- dynamite
- a helicopter
- a spade to tunnel out
- clothes to disguise him as a prison warder
- a giant springboard to leap over the wall
- hide in a laundry basket.

Today's true story from the Bible is about someone who could have escaped from prison, but not using any of these methods.
Come back and tell me:

1. What was his name?
2. How did he escape from his chains?
3. Why did he remain in the prison and not escape?

CONSOLIDATION 2

Mark off an area to be the prison. All the children go to prison and are given a coloured token. One leader acts as gaoler. The leaders have coloured balls or sponges that are the same colours as the tokens. On the command, 'Earthquake!' all the children shout out their colour repeatedly. Leaders throw the coloured balls to the children in the prison. When a child retrieves a ball the same colour as his token he gives both ball and token to the gaoler and is let out of prison. The token is placed in a container and the ball is returned to the leaders for reuse. All children who have been released join the leaders in retrieving and throwing balls to rescue the remaining prisoners.

WIND-UP 2

Remind the children about the warm-up and go over the answers to the questions. How did Paul escape from his chains? Was it by handing in a token? Point out that God was with Paul, even in prison. What happened as a result of Paul going to prison? The gaoler believed in Jesus and was saved.

PAUL'S FINAL JOURNEY

Text: Acts 27:1-44

Teaching Point: God will keep his promises to us, just as he did to Paul.

Memory verse: *God commands all people everywhere to repent. Acts 17:30*

WARM-UP 1

Tell the children you are going on a long journey. Can they suggest ways you could travel? Pin up pictures of their suggestions. Suggested ways are: aeroplane, car, coach, train, bicycle, walk, camel, horse, boat. (See page 88)

Today's true story from the Bible is about someone who had to make a very long journey (Caesarea to Rome is approximately 1380 miles). Come back and tell me:

1. What way did he travel in today's story?
2. What went wrong? or, What was the bad news? [*storm and shipwreck*]
3. What went right? or, What was the good news? [*no one lost their lives*]

CONSOLIDATION 1

Mark out an area down the centre of the room to be the boat. Place lidded containers in the boat, some containing cards with the memory verse written on, others with cards saying, 'The Lord is faithful to all his promises. Psalm 145:13' and the remainder saying, 'God cares for you. 1 Peter 5:7.' The sets of cards should be on 3 different colours.

All the children and leaders get into the boat and sit facing Leader 1 at the front. Leader 1 calls out various commands and the people in the boat perform the appropriate actions.

- Storm - clap hands for thunder.
- Rough water - rock from side to side.
- Cargo overboard - throw all the boxes out of the boat.
- Shipwreck - run to the side of the room with swimming motion and return to the boat.
- Hoist the sail - pull hands down one after the other as though pulling on a rope.
- Collect cargo - collect the boxes back into the boat.

WIND-UP 1

Everyone gets into the boat for the wind-up. Remind the children about the warm-up and go over the answers to the questions. Open up the cargo boxes and separate the cards into their 3 colours. Ask 3 older children to read out one of each colour cards. Remind the children how God kept his promises to and cared for Paul. God is the same today and will keep his promises to us. Read out the cards again.

PAUL'S FINAL JOURNEY

Text: Acts 27:1-44

Teaching Point: God will keep his promises to us, just as he did to Paul.

Memory verse: *God commands all people everywhere to repent. Acts 17:30*

WARM-UP 2

Ask the children to perform various actions in class groups and promise them a reward for doing so. Keep your promise to the younger children, but tell the older children you have changed your mind. They do not get their reward. Do the same with the leaders. Ask the children if you acted fairly? Can they trust you to keep your promises? Hand out the rewards to those who did not get them. Can we trust God to keep his promises?

Today's true story from the Bible is about a situation where it was really important that Paul knew he could trust God to keep his promise. Come back and tell me:

1. What was the situation?
2. What was the promise?

CONSOLIDATION 2

Divide the children into teams. Each team member sits one behind the other in a line. At one end of the line are a number of pieces of paper, rolled into tubes as scrolls. Write one word of the following sentence on 8 of the pieces of paper: '*God can be trusted to keep his promises.*' At the other end of each line is the same number of table tennis balls, or similar, as the total of pieces of paper. Each team sends a scroll down the line and returns a table tennis ball. The scrolls are the message from God to Paul that everyone on the boat would be saved. The table tennis balls are the people escaping safely to land. Once all the scrolls and table tennis balls have changed ends the scrolls are opened and the 8 words put into sentence order. The winning team is the first one to complete the exercise.

WIND-UP 2

Remind the children about the warm-up. Why is it important to know that someone can be trusted to keep their promises? If that person cannot be trusted will people believe what they tell them next time? Go over the answers to the warm-up questions. Refer to the game. What message did God give to Paul? Did God keep his promise? Ask a child to read out the message contained in the scrolls.

THE BIRTH OF JOHN THE BAPTIST

Trudy enters in a rush and looks around.

Trudy Oh, hello, everyone, have you seen Toby? I've got something really exciting to tell him. [*Calls*] Toby! Toby!

I wish he'd hurry up. He must be home from school by now. Can you help me call him? On the count of 3 call, 'Toby! Toby! Where are you?' Ready? One, two, three, Toby! Toby! Where are you?

Toby Is someone calling my name? [*Looks round.*]

Oh, hi everybody. Good to see you all.

Trudy Oh, Toby, am I glad to see you. I've got something really exciting to tell you.

Toby OK Trudy, just cool it. What is it?

Trudy You know my friend Jemima?

Toby [*Looks towards the ceiling and back*] Only too well.

Trudy Really, Toby, you're always being mean about Jemima. What's she ever done to you?

Toby She's just soppy, Trudy. Still, I suppose like attracts like.

Trudy If you're going to be rude I shan't tell you my news.

Toby Oh, come on, Trudy, don't be so silly. I was only teasing. What's the news?

Trudy Well, Jemima came to school this morning and, guess what?

Toby What?

Trudy Her mum's had her baby.

Toby Hope it doesn't look like Jemima.

Trudy Why not?

Toby 'Cos she looks like a monkey, that's why not.

Trudy No she doesn't!

Toby Yes she does!

Trudy Well I don't think she does. I think she's really pretty.

Toby OK, OK. If you think she's really pretty, we'll say she's really pretty. [*Shakes his head at the audience*]

Trudy Jemima said the baby's ever so sweet.

Toby looks as though he might be sick.

Trudy She held him in her arms.

Toby What's his name?

Trudy They don't know yet.

Toby You can't have a baby without a name.

Trudy Jemima said they hadn't made up their minds yet. Her mum likes one thing and her dad another.

Toby Why can't they make up their minds?

Trudy Jemima said her mum wants to call him Toby.

Toby What's wrong with that? I think Toby is a great name to have.

Trudy Jemima said her dad doesn't think he looks like a Toby. Her dad thinks he looks more like a Richard.

Toby Um, sounds a bit odd to me. How can you look like a name?

Trudy I don't know. Never mind about his name. Jemima said he's absolutely perfect. Her mum thinks so, too. She heard her mum tell her dad she was sure he was going to do something really special when he grows up.

Toby Honestly, Trudy, Jemima's family must be nuts. They have a baby. They think he looks like a name. And they're already planning what he's going to do when he grows up! Crazy!

Toby exits, shaking his head.

Trudy Well I don't think they're crazy. I wish my mum would have a new baby. I bet he'd be even more special than Jemima's baby brother. [*Exits*]

GOD'S GIFT TO MARY

Trudy enters and looks round.

Trudy Hello, how are you? I've had a really fantastic day. Everything went well. I got all my spellings right. And my teacher said I'm really clever. Not like Toby. He never does as well as me.

Toby enters carrying a letter.

Toby Hey, Trudy, look what I've got.

Trudy What?

Toby This letter. I got it at school.

Trudy What's it about? Let me see!

Toby Hang on and I'll read it to you. Dear Toby, I am pleased to inform you that you have been selected to represent your county in the under 13s football match on Saturday, (*a date 2-3 months in the future*).

Trudy Hey, Toby, that sounds brilliant. What does it mean?

Toby I asked my teacher. She said it means I'm on the county football team.

Trudy You! On the county football team? Are you sure?

Toby It does sound a bit funny, doesn't it?

Trudy I suppose you could be good enough. After all, you're always playing football. And you are in the school team.

Toby Yes, that's true. But no one else has had a letter.

Trudy So what else does it say?

Toby It says I have to go for training.

Trudy When?

Toby Every week. On a Tuesday at 6 o'clock.

Trudy But that's tonight. You'd better get ready or you'll be late.

Toby But what if it's not true? If I turn up for training and the letter's not true, I'll look silly.

Trudy Why do you think it's not true? The letter looks true.

Toby I know. I just don't want to look silly.

Trudy Your teacher thinks it's true.

Toby Yes. But I'm just not sure.

Trudy Can you phone the person who wrote it tomorrow to check?

Toby The trouble is, the letter says if I don't turn up for training I'll lose my place.

Trudy Oh dear.

Toby What shall I do?

Trudy The letter sounds true.

Toby Yes.

Trudy Your teacher thinks it's true.

Toby Yes.

Trudy You're good at football.

Toby Yes.

Trudy So why don't you believe it?

Toby I don't know really.

Trudy Well, if you want to be in the team you've got to go to training, so make up your mind. Do you believe the letter, or not?

Toby I want to believe it, Trudy. But I'm just not sure. [*Exits*]

Trudy I do hope he doesn't miss out. [*Exits*]

SIMON AND THE WOMAN

A half empty box of chocolates is on a table in clear view of the audience.

Trudy [*Enters singing*]. Oh, hello, girls and boys, it's very nice to see you. My name's Trudy. Have you seen my brother Toby? Dad wants him.

Can you help me call him? On the count of 3 call, 'Toby! Toby! Where are you?' Ready? One, two, three, Toby! Toby! Where are you?

Toby What do **you** want? [*Looks round.*]

Oh, hello boys and girls. Good to see you all.

Trudy Dad wants to see you. He's ever so cross. He's got steam coming out of his ears.

Toby Why?

Trudy He found the new chocolate box half empty this morning. **And** he knows you've had them.

Toby But you had one too!

Trudy Yes, well that's different. **I** only had **one**, but **you** had at **least** 10.

Toby So? You did wrong too.

Trudy No I didn't. I only had one chocolate, **and** I've been working really hard at school, **and** Dad said he'd give me a reward, so I deserved the chocolate. You didn't.

Toby How does Dad know I took them? Did you tell on me?

Trudy I didn't need to. Dad knew it was you, 'cos you're always naughty.

Toby What do you think he'll do?

Trudy Something really bad, I expect. He sent me to find you. He said you've got to go and see him straight away. Now.

Toby Oooh, I hope he's not too angry. Do I really have to go?

Trudy Yes! Immediately! Dad is so angry his glasses have steamed up.

Toby I don't want to go. Dad's always really cross when I do anything wrong. Oooh! Do you think if I hide he might forget?

Trudy Dad says you have to go. Now! After all, you did take the chocolates.

Toby I suppose I did. I'd better go and find Dad and say sorry. I don't really want to. Are you coming too?

Trudy Why should I come?

Toby Well you took one too.

Trudy That's different. I only took one. And I deserved it for working hard, so I don't need to say sorry.

Toby Oh well, I'd better go and find Dad and get it over with. [*Exits*]

Trudy [smugly] I expect Dad will stop his pocket money for a whole year. Serve him right. He's always being naughty. He deserves to be punished. I never do anything wrong. And I work hard at school. Toby doesn't. His teachers are always saying he could do better.

Toby [*Enters quietly with head down.*]

Trudy So? What did he say? Have you lost your pocket money? Has Dad stopped you going out?

Toby No. I went and owned up and said I was really sorry and I wouldn't do it again. And guess what?

Trudy What?

Toby Dad forgave me.

Trudy But what punishment did he give you?

Toby Nothing. He just said not to do it again.

Trudy [*Jumping up and down*] That's not fair. Why should you get away with it? Just because you said sorry. And I bet you didn't really mean it.

Toby Yes, I did. And you took a chocolate as well, Trudy, so you ought to go and say sorry to Dad, too.

Trudy But I only took one. And I'm not naughty like you, Toby, so I don't need to say sorry.

Toby Well, I think you should. After all, you did take a chocolate, even though you didn't take as many as me. Dad'll forgive you if you say sorry. He did me, and I took 10 chocolates.

Trudy Listen, clothhead, I don't need to say sorry. [*Flounces off*]

Toby But taking one was still wrong. You need to say sorry too. [*Exits*]

Leader *Does Trudy need to be forgiven as well? Today's true story from the Bible will help you work out the answer. Listen carefully and come back and tell me whether Trudy needs to say sorry as well.*

THE GOOD SAMARITAN

Perform the script with a puppet or soft toy. The puppet squeaks or nods after each statement made by the leader.

LEADER: This is my friend, Jemima. Jemima really likes me, don't you Jemima? *(Puppet nods/ squeaks.)*

LEADER: Jemima says I'm her best friend. *(Puppet nods.)*

LEADER: Do you know what she told me? She's always going to be my friend. *(Puppet nods.)*

LEADER: She's coming to school with me. *(Puppet nods.)*

LEADER: She'll always play with me at playtime. *(Puppet nods.)*

[Leader asks the children what sorts of things friends do. Following each suggestion the leader says, 'Will you do that Jemima?' Each time puppet nods and squeaks.)

LEADER: I'm so happy that you're going to be my friend. *(Puppet squeaks.)*

LEADER: We're going to my house for tea, aren't we Jemima? *(Puppet nods.)*

(Another squeaky puppet appears over the board and squeaks. Jemima looks around and squeaks.)

LEADER: What's going on, Jemima? *(Puppet squeaks as though explaining something.)*

LEADER: Jemima says that Percy has asked her to go to the cinema with him. But what about going to my house? *(Puppet squeaks.)*

LEADER: Jemima says she'd rather go with Percy.

Leader asks the children if Jemima behaved like a real friend?

AUTHORITY TO SAVE

Enter Trudy.

Trudy Good morning, popsicles.

Toby [*off stage, getting louder with each word*] List! List! List!

Trudy [*surprised with head on one* side] I'm listening.

Toby [*off stage*] List! [*pause*] List! [*pause*]

Trudy [*changes head to the other side*] I'm still listening.

Enter Toby.

Toby What are you doing, Trudy?

Trudy I'm listening - just like you said.

Toby Are you kwaaazy, you mushroom head?

Trudy You say, 'List', I say, 'Beethoven'.

Toby You are kwaaazy - or concussed.

Trudy You shouted out 6 times [*stops to count*] 5 times, [*at top of her voice*] 'List'

Toby No, no, no! I mean birthday list.

Trudy Whose birthday list?

Toby Myyy birthday list. I'm going to be 12 one day soon and mum and dad said I could invite my friends to a party.

Trudy Who have you got so far? Perhaps (*Leader's name*) could write the names down for us?

Leader *writes the names on a flipchart or board.*

Toby Well, there's Timmy Jessop. He's my second best friend and he is granite.

Trudy Granite?

Toby Yeah, tough and grey.

Trudy Who else?

Toby Mark And [*pause*] erson.

Trudy Because?

Toby He's clever.

Trudy That's two. How many more?

Toby John Phillips, because he's a great swimmer. Alex Place, because his father is rich. David Taylor, because he's cool. Andy Jones, because he's great at sport. And Micky Drago.

Trudy Who's Micky Drago?

Toby The new boy. You know, the one who started a few weeks ago.

Trudy But he's not one of us.

Toby What do you mean?

Trudy He doesn't come from around here.

Toby You mean, he comes from (*a nearby town*)?

Trudy No, you big drop kick! He comes from another country, another tribe, another people.

Toby Why's that so bad?

Trudy He's from .... They're just not like us from over there. They do things wrong and they're rude and ugly.

Toby But didn't they beat us at tennis last week, cricket the week before that, rugby last month and swimming - oooh - they always beat us at swimming don't they?

Trudy That's just because they cheat. And anyway - haven't you noticed... Micky's feet smell, he has no breeding. There is more culture in a tub of yoghurt than there is in all his family!

Toby I suppose you're right. We don't want any outsiders.

Trudy That's right Toby. Just stick to the people you know.

Toby That's settled then. No outsiders, no people who are different. I'll only invite people who will fit in - and give me great presents! Boy, this is going to be a dyno party - fun, food, friends ... *and no girls!*

Toby exits, followed by Trudy.

SIMILIFIED PASSOVER MEAL

Sit in groups of 10-12 in a circle, with the candle in the centre. The leader's comments are in italic.

1. Recall the search for yeast and its removal. Explain 'unleavened bread'.

2. Light the candle.

    Blessed are you, Lord God, who created light.

3. Fill the cup with red juice (first cup).

    God said: 'I will bring you out from under the burdens of the Egyptians.' Blessed are you, Lord God, King of the universe.

    Pass round the cup.

4. Dip parsley in the bowl of salt water.

    Remember the hyssop dipped in the blood of the lamb, which was painted on the lintel and doorposts.

5. Break the middle matzah in half and put half to one side on a napkin. Hold up the other half.

    This is the bread of slavery, which our fathers ate in the land of Egypt.

    Replace with other 2 matzot.

6. Fill the cup with red juice (second cup).

    God said: 'I will deliver you from being slaves.'

7. Youngest present asks -

    Why is this night different from all other nights?

    Reply -

    We were slaves to Pharaoh in Egypt, and the Lord our God brought us out with a mighty hand and an outstretched arm. If God had not brought us out we would still be Pharaoh's slaves.

8. Point to the various items on the table.

    What is the meaning of the lamb? It is the sacrifice of the Lord's Passover when he passed over our houses and killed the Egyptians.

    What is the meaning of the unleavened bread? Our fathers baked unleavened bread because they were thrust out of Egypt and could not wait.

    What is the meaning of the bitter herbs? The Egyptians made our fathers' lives bitter with all kinds of hard work.

9. Raise the second cup of red juice.

    We thank you, O Lord, for delivering us from slavery.

    Pass round the cup.

10. Break the upper and middle half matzah into the required number of portions for each person in the group.

    Bless you, O Lord our God, King of the universe.

    Pass round.

11. Pick up bitter herbs and charoset.

    Blessed are you, O Lord our God, King of the universe.

    Dip watercress into the charoset, passing from person to person.

12. Break the lower matzah into the required number of portions and distribute with the remaining watercress. Pass round the lamb.

13. Break the remaining half matzah and distribute.

14. Fill the cup with red juice (third cup).

    God said: 'I will redeem you with an outstretched arm'. Blessed are you, O Lord our God, King of the universe.

    Pass round the cup.

15. Fill the cup with red juice (fourth cup).

    God said: 'I will take you to me for a people'. Thank you, Lord God, that you are our King and our Saviour.

    Pass round the cup.

16. *The remembrance of the Passover is now complete.*

POWER PROMISED

Trudy [*Singing*]. Hello, girls and boys, it's nice to see you. Are you having a good day? I am.

Toby enters while Trudy is talking.

Toby Hi, Trudy. You sound happy.

Trudy Ooh, I am. In fact, I'm so happy I could kiss you. [*Gives Toby a kiss on the cheek*]

Toby Ugh, get off, Trudy. Anyway, what are you so happy about?

Trudy My class is going to vote for a new prefect tomorrow.

Toby So?

Trudy I'm in the running.

Toby You? Who put your name forward?

Trudy My friend, Jemima. **And** Miss said I should do it.

Toby I always knew your class was crazy, Trudy, and now they've proved it. You? Standing for class prefect?

Trudy You're just jealous. I bet no one in your class has asked you to be a prefect.

Toby Pooh, who wants to be a prefect. So, how many are up for it? All the class?

Trudy No, just 4 of us.

Toby Well, I suppose Jemima will vote for you, and maybe Susie.

Trudy It's not just friends who vote for you, Toby.

Toby So, who else votes for you apart from friends?

Trudy We all have to make a speech, telling everyone what we will do if we are elected. Then everyone votes for the person they think will do the best job.

Toby Ah, I see. And what are you going to say.

Trudy I shall promise to arrange a Christmas party for the class.

Toby Are you sure you can do that? It takes a lot of time and hard work.

Trudy Of course I can. I'll promise everyone a chocolate egg at Easter. Then they'll vote for me.

Toby Are you sure you can do that? Where will you get the money?

Trudy Dad'll give it to me. Don't you worry.

Toby Umm, I'm not sure about that, Trudy. What else?

Trudy And I shall promise to give everyone an extra day's holiday in the summer.

Toby Trudy. You can't promise that. There's no way you can keep that promise.

Trudy Pshaw! And I will make sure no one will have to do games, **and** all the teachers will be nice to us, **and** no one will get a detention, **and** we'll have chocolate pudding every Friday.

Toby Trudy, do you know what you've been saying? You're promising things you can't do.

Trudy That's what you think. When they hear **my** speech **everyone** will vote for me.

Trudy flounces off.

Toby Not even Trudy's class can be that stupid, surely? Oh dear. I'm glad I'm going out to tea tomorrow. [*Exits*]

PETER IN PRISON

A suitcase and clothing, etc. is strewn around the area. Trudy enters and looks at the mess.

Trudy Oh, dear, how am I going to get all this into my suitcase? I need some help.

Toby enters.

Toby Are you ready, Trudy? I'm all packed and ready to go.

Trudy [*sadly*] Oh, Toby, I don't know how I'm going to get all this packed up.

Toby Don't worry, I'll help. [*Leader's name*] will help too. Let's get the suitcase out.

Trudy How do I know what to put in it?

Toby You must pack everything you'll need while you're away. But it's only going to be 3 days.

Trudy I suppose so. Will you help me?

Toby OK. Let's start with clothes. You'll need tee-shirts. [*to audience*] How many? 2 or 3?

Toby And some jeans. [*Leader or actors packs the Tshirts and jeans.*]

Trudy What about socks? I like lots of socks. [*Pack socks*]

Toby And a jumper. [*Pack jumper*]

Trudy And my pyjamas. [*Pack some pyjamas*]

Toby Don't forget the shoes. [*Packs shoes*]

Trudy Or my underwear. [*Packs underwear*]

Toby What else? [*Ask the children, prompt if necessary... toiletries, towel, swimming things.*]

Toby That looks about right.

Trudy But there's nothing for me to read. And what about my Bible?

Toby Well remembered, Trudy. [*Pack comics and Bible*]

Toby Right, that's finished. Oh, Trudy, I'm really excited about this trip. It will be such fun.

Trudy I hope so.

Toby Of course it will. It'll be great.

Trudy But I've never been away without Mum and Dad before.

Toby Aren't you looking forward to it?

Trudy I'm frightened.

Toby What about?

Trudy Say I don't like the food?

Toby Don't worry. Sam told us the food will be nice. He went last year, so he should know.

Trudy But what if I can't keep up with the others?

Toby Don't worry. I'll be there to help you.

Trudy And what if I have bad dreams?

Toby I'll be there too, Trudy. I'll look after you.

Trudy And what if I fall over and hurt myself?

Toby I'll be with you, Trudy. I'll make sure someone puts a plaster on for you.

Trudy But what if …

Toby [*interupts*] Trudy, whatever happens, I will be there and I will help you. Come on, the coach should be arriving any minute. [*Toby and Trudy exit.*]

Contents (in Bible order)

Contents (in OTW for 3-9s order)

Subject Index

Subject Index

Visual Aids for The Birth of Jesus (continued on to page 84)

Lesson 5 Page 14

Shepherds

Joseph with Mary on a donkey

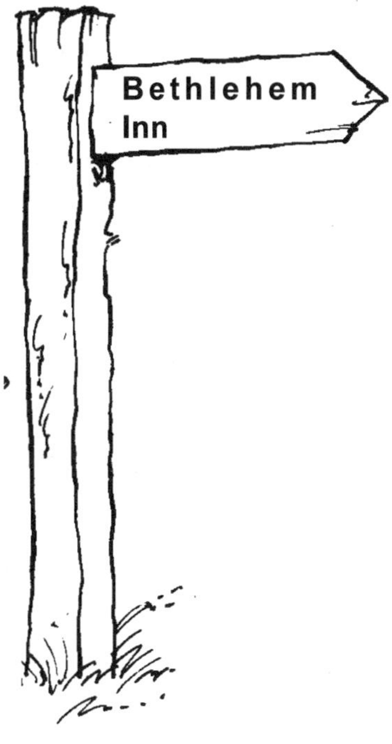

Visual aid for Paul at Philippi Lesson 36/ page 61

Ten Lepers Lesson 28 Page 34

Visual Aids for The Birth of Jesus (continued from page 83) Lesson 5 Page 14

To make a crowd of angels photocopy this as often as needed.

Visual aid for God's Gift to
Simeon Lesson 7/ page 16

Visual aid for The Last
Supper Lesson 25 page 42

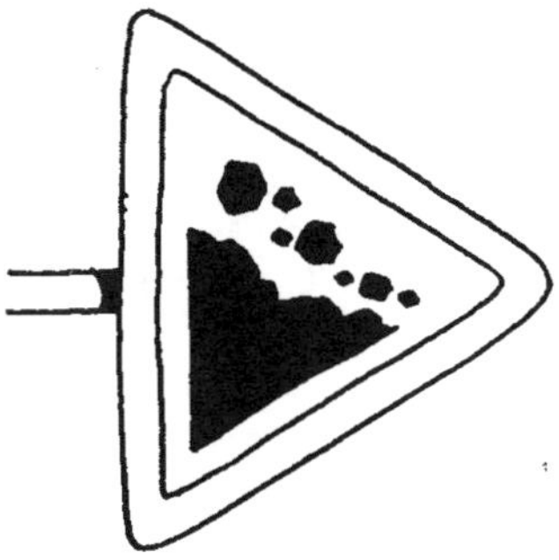

Visual aid for The Crippled Woman
Lesson 15/ page 27

Crowd Scene Visual aid for The Birth of John the Baptist Lesson 1 page 7

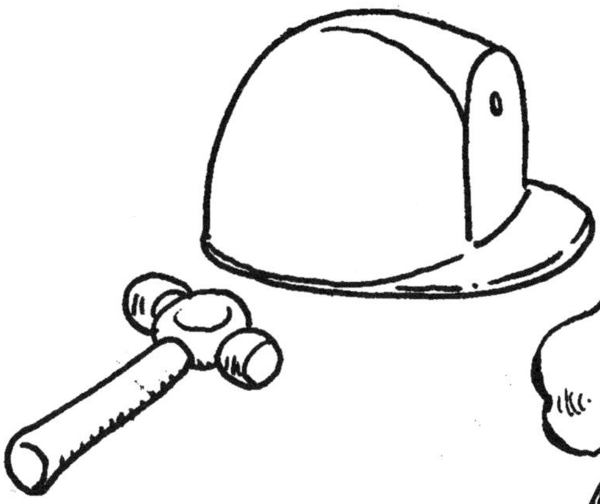

Visual aids for Preparing People for the Message Lesson 3 Page 10

Visual aid for Palm Sunday Lesson 24 Page 40 and

Paul's Final Journey Lesson 38 Page 64

(Elephant on page 91; Tractor and Taxi on page 92; Donkey; Fire Engine and Police car on page 93)

Visual aid for The Birth of Jesus Lesson 5/ page 14

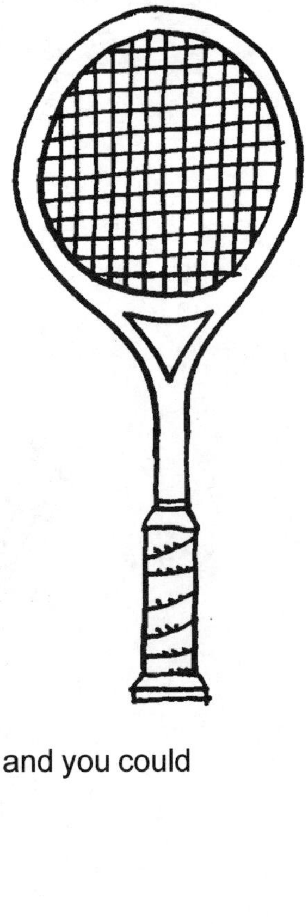

Visual aids for Jesus Calls The First Disciples. Lesson 9. Page 19 and you could use the farmer for Humility in Prayer. Lesson 22. Page 38.

Visual aids for Jesus Calls The First Disciples. Lesson 9. Page 19.

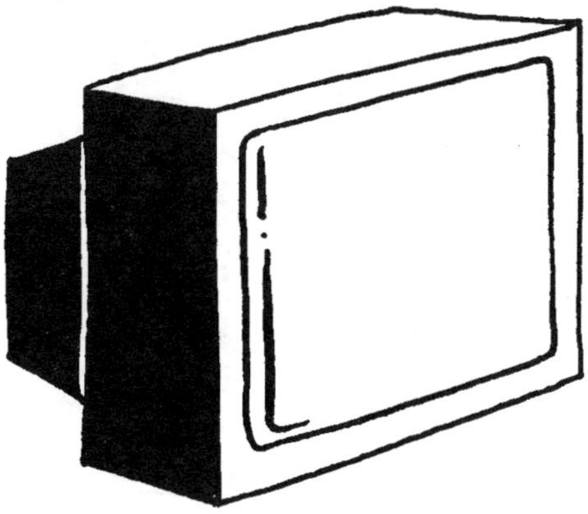

Soldiers and Sailors - Visual aids for Preparing People for the Message Lesson 3 page 10 and Humility in Prayer. Lesson 22. Page 38.

Visual aids for Jesus Calls The First Disciples. Lesson 9. Page 19.

Visual aid for Humility in Prayer. Lesson 22. Page 38.

Visual aid for Humility in Prayer. Lesson 22. Page 38.

Visual aid for Palm Sunday Lesson 24 Page 40 and

Paul's Final Journey Lesson 38 Page 64

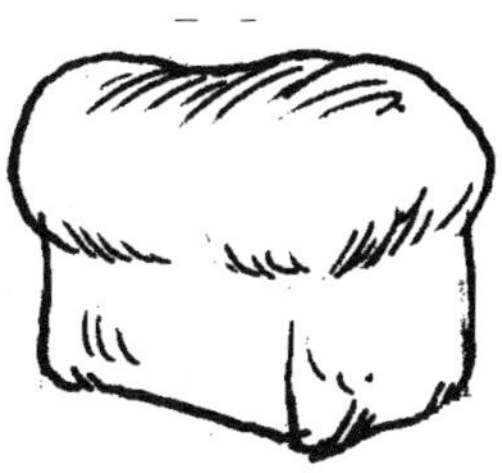

Visual aids for The Last Supper. Lesson 25. Page 42.

The Game is Up
OLD TESTAMENT
Book 1 and Book 2

Take the Bible seriously and have loads of fun while you are at it!

Are you looking to add another dimension to your teaching? Do you want to encourage your children to read the Bible? Do you want them to have strong Biblical foundations without compromising on fun and activity? TnT have developed The Game Is Up for this very purpose.

All the games are directly linked to the lessons with strong Biblical emphasis that covers all major Christian doctrines. Visual aids for photocopying and clearly explained teaching points make this an excellent addition to any church resource library.

Book 1: Genesis, Exodus, Numbers and Joshua.

Book 2: Judges, Ruth, 1 & 2 Samuel, 1 & 2 Kings, 2 Chronicles, Nehemiah, Esther, Job, Jeremiah, Daniel, Jonah.

* The successful On the Way series continued with extra games and activities.
* Book 1: 80 game selections;
* Book 2: 96 game selections
* Flexible enough to be used with any curriculum
* Strong Biblical Emphasis
* Multi age (3-11s)
* Ideal for Holiday Bible Club; Vacation Bible School

The Game is Up
NEW TESTAMENT
Book 3 and Book 4

Take the bible seriously and have loads of fun while you are at it!

This will add another dimension to your teaching, encouraging the children to read the Bible and have firm foundations without compromising on fun and activity.

'The Game Is Up' clearly explains the teaching points, covers all major Christian doctrines and is reproducible. There are visual aids, puppet sketches and scripts.

Book 3: Matthew, Mark and John.

Book 4: Luke and Acts.

QUOTES

Biblical ignorance is a plague not only in the land but in the churches. This material will cure the problem by giving children firm foundations in scriptural knowledge from their earliest years.

Dick Lucas
St. Helen's Bishopgate

CHRISTIAN FOCUS

Good Books with the Real Message of Hope

Christian Focus Publications publishes books for adults and children under its three main imprints: Christian Focus, Mentor and Christian Heritage. Our books reflect that God's word is reliable and Jesus is the way to know him, and live forever with him.

Our children's publication list includes a Sunday school curriculum that covers pre-school to early teens; puzzle and activity books. We also publish personal and family devotional titles, biographies and inspirational stories that children will love.

If you are looking for quality Bible teaching for children then we have an excellent range of Bible story and age specific theological books.

From pre-school to teenage fiction, we have it covered!

Find us at our web page: www.christianfocus.com

THE ONE WAY

TnT

TnT Ministries (which stands for Teaching and Training Ministries) was launched in February 1993 by Christians from a broad variety of denominational backgrounds who are concerned that teaching the Bible to children be taken seriously. The leaders were in charge of a Sunday School of 50 teachers at St Helen's Bishopgate, an evangelical church in the city of London, for 13 years, during which time a range of Biblical teaching material has been developed. TnT Ministries also runs training days for Sunday School teachers.